Bells, Gongs, and Wooden Fish

無聲息的歌唱

Bells, Gongs and Wooden Fish

VOICES FOR BUDDHIST CHANGE

Venerable Master Hsing Yun

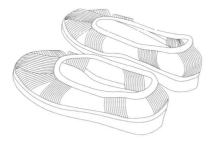

Buddha's Light Publishing, Los Angeles

© 2012 Buddha's Light Publishing
First edition

By Venerable Master Hsing Yun
Originally published in Chinese 《無聲息的歌唱》
Photograph by Ming-Ying Zhuang
Cover designed by John Gill

Published by Buddha's Light Publishing
3456 S. Glenmark Drive
Hacienda Heights, CA 91745, U.S.A.
Tel: (626) 923-5144
Fax: (626) 923-5145
E-mail: itc@blia.org
Website: www.blpusa.com

Printed in Taiwan.

Library of Congress Cataloging-in-Publication Data

Xingyun, da shi.
   [Wu sheng xi de ge chang. English]
   Bells, gongs, and wooden fish : voices for Buddhist change / Venerable Master Hsing Yun.
-- 1st ed.
      pages cm
   Includes bibliographical references.
   ISBN 978-1-932293-70-8
   1. Buddhist renewal. I. Title. II. Title: Voices for Buddhist change.

BQ9800.F6392X557513 2012
294.3'92--dc23

                        2012012594

Contents

Acknowledgments

Like all of Buddha's Light Publishing's endeavors, this project benefited from the contributions of many people. We would like to thank Venerable Tzu Jung, the Chief Executive of the Fo Guang Shan International Translation Center (FGSITC), Venerble Hui Chi, Abbot of Hsi Lai Temple, and Venerable Yi Chao, Director of FGSITC for their support and leadership.

Bill and Cathy Maher, Robert Smitheram, Echo Tsai, Stuart Pollock, Stephanie Hong, Anne Tung, Jacqueline Leung and Amanda Ling provided the translation. John Gill and Susan Tidwell edited the texts; Louvenia Ortega and Nathan Michon proofread the manuscript and prepared it for publication. Photographs and illustrations provided by Gandha Samudra Culture Company and Ming-Ying Zhuang. The book was designed by Wan Kah Ong and the cover was designed by John Gill.

Our appreciation goes to everyone who supported this project from conception to completion.

Foreword

If one were to make a short list of the most defining and enduring characteristics that mark the career of Venerable Master Hsing Yun, the list would most certainly have to include reform and innovation. Reform germinates in courage, and innovation grows from creativity. To conceive of and compose *Bells, Gongs, and Wooden Fish: Voices for Buddhist Change* took no less than this—a courageous heart and an innovative mind. In retrospect, the personal risk to the budding reputation and career of a twenty-four-year-old promoter of the Dharma cannot be understated. A suspicious post-war political climate had spread throughout Taiwan. Refugees from mainland China had inundated the small island and caused a scarcity of resources, including food and shelter for the monks who came both as refugees and as medical aid workers, It was a perilous act to criticize the so called hand that fed you. Reflecting upon this helps one to understand the significance and timeliness of these bold and imaginative memoirs—seventeen personified voices of Buddhist liturgical instruments and other objects of monastic life—collected in this unique book.

From humble beginnings as a twelve-year-old novice monk in a 1,350-year-old temple on the outskirts of Nanjing, China during a harrowing time of war, Hsing Yun would go on to become a beloved Buddhist leader, a renowned Dharma teacher, innovative modernizer of the means of delivering the Buddhist message, humanitarian, and philanthropist. He would also become a prolific writer of more than one hundred books, ranging from the didactic and historical to the literary and inspirational. His books have been translated into a myriad of languages. Throughout all of the Dharma propagation projects that Hsing Yun has envisioned and undertaken around the globe, a spirit of daring reform and a boundless zeal for forward-thinking and creative energy has marked every one of his efforts. Looking back over the span of this illustrious and lengthy career, *Bells, Gongs, and Wooden Fish: Voices for Buddhist Change*, though a brief composition in comparison to the works that would follow, embarks bravely—like the pair of monastic shoes described in the text—upon a journey toward innovative reform.

Written individually between the years of 1951 and 1953, these sketches were collected into Hsing Yun's second book-length publication, and they immediately received attention as an upstart, clarion call to the Chinese Buddhist community—both leaders and followers alike—to reform Buddhism before it "withered away". The young Hsing Yun had, just two years before, fled mainland China leading a group of monks on a medical relief mission to Taiwan. Tens of thousands of refugees were flooding onto the small island as China's civil war was ending. Times were uncertain, and he had been struggling to find both a new spiritual home and one that would sustain his daily needs in the mundane world. Monastic refugees, too, abounded in Taiwan at that time, and resources were scarce. As Hsing Yun himself recounts, he had to sell his "youthful vigor" for food. That is to say, being young and strong, and quite fit and large in stature, he worked at manual labor, such as hauling wood, water, and even corpses. A less intellectual challenge than he most likely desired, he, nevertheless, did whatever was necessary.

In 1951, Master Miaoguo of Yuanguang Temple in Chungli, where he had finally found shelter, took him south to Miaoli to oversee an area of dense jungle around Fayun Temple on Mt. Guanyin. The area was part of Fayun Temple's landholdings, but poachers were known to hunt the small animals that lived in the jungle. Master Miaoguo was renovating Fayun Temple's main hall, as it had suffered much damage in a devastating earthquake that had occurred in 1935. Timber was being harvested from the jungle to be used for renovation, and this needed to be guarded from the poachers. Charged to watch over the forest, Hsing Yun was installed in a grass hut on the mountain, and meals were taken up to him daily.

In such isolation, Hsing Yun began to see his youth slipping away before him, passing by without a chance to implement his growing list of ideas for promoting the Dharma. He also began to see how Chinese Buddhism had been languishing for centuries as either a funeral-centered or a ghost-centered religion, essentially out of touch with the day-to-day spiritual needs of the people. The young, idealistic monk realized that in order for Buddhism to be revived, the many cultural superstitions that had overgrown Buddhism's focus and were choking the life out of it had to be hacked away so that light could reach the long-shaded areas between the tangled branches and the tree of the Dharma could once again be healthy and vital. In other words, Buddhism must again become universally relevant and practical for people in their daily lives.

Hsing Yun had been deeply influenced by the Buddhist activist and modernist Master Taixu (太虛 1890-1947). In fact, as a young monk studying at Jiaoshan Buddhist College, he attended a leadership seminar given by Taixu. This was most likely the awakening of his reformer's heart. Later the young monk would vow to continue the work of reforming Chinese Buddhism that Taixu had initiated. In the years to follow, Hsing Yun would publish scores of books on his insights into the teachings of the Buddha: translations of and commentaries on the classical sutras, Chan poems and *gongan* adaptations, pragmatic treatises on incorporating the wisdom of Buddhism into daily life, inspirational works on Humanistic Buddhism, magazine articles, and newspaper columns. He even composed songs and developed dramas for television and the stage, all the while placing the utmost faith in the efficacy of the written word to express and promote the teachings of the Dharma. As impressive as is his canon of later works, *Bells, Gongs, and Wooden Fish: Voices for Buddhist Change* most certainly represents an early turning point in his career.

This second major work of Hsing Yun has been referred to in other texts as *Song of Silence*, but it has not previously been translated and published in the English language. This title, while useful, fails to adequately convey the true and deeper meaning of the Chinese title, *wu shengxi de gechang* (無聲息的歌唱). The term "silence" connotes the action of listening; it is an action of listening to that which is not heard. It is a passive action that a listener does. However, the personalities of the personified Dharma instruments and the objects in these sketches themselves sing out. These are the songs of their hearts—notes that have heretofore gone unheard and unheeded—singing from the pages. It is their inexpressible melodies that the young Hsing Yun harkens to and gives voice to for us, the reader, to hear. Thus, the more concrete title *Bells, Gongs, and Wooden Fish: Voices for Buddhist Change* has been chosen to give a more descriptive idea to readers as to the book's contents.

It is not surprising that this "silence" was heard by the ears of youth, for it is so often the case that only the ears of the young are still intimately tuned to the direct experience of life, that the ardent and spirited imagination of youth is not yet bridled and tamed by life's more utilitarian toils. These songs were heard by an inspired, hardworking—and most likely lonely—young monk in a small, thatched hut in a dense forest on a remote mountainside. The songs of the Dharma instruments and other items of Buddhist temple life are the songs of his closest friends singing out to him during the long, solitary nights spent on the mountain. With no overtones of a human voice to drown out the constants of daily monastic life, the pure notes of the Dharma were able to ring out. By lantern light, Hsing Yun would record them on scraps of paper, as if transcribing a symphony onto a musical staff.

What are these songs that Hsing Yun heard? They are the untold histories of the exhaltations and exploitations of the Dharma instruments and things dear to monastic life. They are the impassioned strains of their trials and tribulations that Hsing Yun both celebrates and laments on their behalf. They are the lyrics, ballads, hymns, odes, and elegies of daily life lived according to the Buddha's teachings. Finally, they are the melodies of a receptive and sensitive young monk's world, illuminating the inexpressibly wondrous beauty he longs to share with others, yet there is a strain of discordance that runs through the profound polyphony.

Bells, Gongs, and Wooden Fish: Voices for Buddhist Change is first and foremost Hsing Yun's declaration of reform. He was making his stand. It is a value that we here in the West hold so dear, know so well, and solemnly take to heart; the ideology of reform is part of our very fiber. This is one of the reasons, I believe, Western readers can connect so effortlessly with Hsing Yun. Even in the very first sketch, "Big Bell," he reveals to us the wellspring of his inspiration: liberty. He makes the connection between freedom, liberty, and the Buddhist concept of liberation. He chooses to have Big Bell observe a monastic holding a magazine with a picture of the Liberty Bell on the cover. Big Bell immediately recognizes the Liberty Bell and calls to mind the United States of America's Declaration of Independence. Similarly, *Bells, Gongs, and Wooden Fish: Voices for Buddhist Change* is Hsing Yun's "declaration" of Buddhist freedom, freedom from the corruption and degradation into which Chinese Buddhism had spiraled. However, as idealistic as he is, he is foremost a pragmatist. What was needed? The first step would be for Buddhists to admit their faults and talk about them. This is what *Bells, Gongs, and Wooden Fish: Voices for Buddhist Change* signifies: a painful but necessary first step toward change. In going back to this point in time and looking forward, it is astonishing to see what a watershed moment of change this book was!

Bells, Gongs, and Wooden Fish: Voices for Buddhist Change is also a delightful read. The chapters skillfully balance profundity and inventive personification. The Buddhist liturgical instruments and other sacred items are characterized with lighthearted charm and speak to us with very individual personalities. As they begin to tell their stories, one hears both tunes of eager exuberance and sincere gratitude in their words at their chance to introduce themselves. It is only after they start to reveal themselves that one begins to get a sense that there is more happening here. As is so distinct to the Chan way of communicating, there is much said in the wordlessness between the lines. One by one, as they each sing out, they tell of the sorrows and outrage associated with the corruption and diminishment of Chinese Buddhism. It is the age-old song of the degradation of Buddhist practices, loss of tradition, and respect for the liturgy. Still, each song is underscored by a rhythm of hopefulness. Hsing Yun is in no way a fundamentalist, but these sketches repeatedly call for a purification of Buddhist practices in order to revive Buddhism.

This English language version of *wu shengxi de gechang* makes two substantial changes from the original that was published in Taiwan: first, only seventeen of the original twenty sketches are included; second, a brief article precedes each sketch. Three of the sketches have been omitted, because the items were felt to be culturally awkward and quite obscure nowadays. It was also felt that some brief, explanatory information about each of the items would help the reader better understand the role each object plays in Buddhist religious life.

In reading these stories, we are reminded of how, if we each would open ourselves intimately to all that surrounds us in our daily lives, we, too, could hear the deep insights they are communicating to us. This, I believe, is the deepest message of Master Hsing Yun's teachings of Humanistic Buddhism. This is surely the silent melody of his own heart, which he has been voicing for over six decades for all to hear. If we but listen!

Susan Tidwell
Hsi Lai Temple

Preface

Bells, Gongs, and Wooden Fish: Voices for Buddhist Change contains twenty[1] sketches that were written hastily and with little emphasis on organization during a two-year period of my life not long after I had arrived in Taiwan. Beginning in 1951, they were published serially in two monthly magazines, first in *Awakening Life* (覺生) and then in *Bodhi Tree* (菩提樹). The sketches were written to present the liturgical Dharma instruments of Chinese Buddhism and other traditional objects of ritual and daily monastic life. I have allowed the instruments and objects to speak for themselves, revealing their own unique stories—often majestic and sometimes tragic—in, as it were, personified memoirs.

In the spring of 1946, I employed this same style for an article entitled "Money Talks" that was published in the *New Jiangsu Newspaper*. I had come to realize that the goal of literature was to convey one's feelings and ideas, and I believed that this writing technique could bring those feelings and ideas to life in a very vivid and expressive way. While I was writing these sketches, I drew on no direct inspiration from anyone; I simply thought that this style of writing could be very effective.

Originally, I had felt no haste in compiling these twenty sketches into a collection, since they had all been published previously, and especially when I thought about the conditions that allowed me to publish them in the first place. Even now, I am quite

---

1. Seventeen sketches have been included in the English language edition. *Ed.*

moved by the fortuitous occurrence of events. It was while writing my fourteenth sketch that I received an unexpected, yet happy surprise. My beloved, former master, Cihang (慈航), sent me a sum of money. Accompanying these funds was a letter. He wrote, "Your 'stories'? Are you still writing them? I have sent you some money so you can hurry up and publish them!" During those years of hardship, a poor, young monk like me wouldn't have dared to dream about writing and publishing a book of his own. That was wishful thinking. But this master's compassion and care reached me in the remote place where I was staying at that time. How can I ever live up to the kindness of this elder? As a result, not long after my translation of the *Commentary on the Universal Gate Sutra* had been published, I was able once again to connect with readers through this collection of sketches.

I regret that the content of these sketches is not as polished and substantial as I would have liked, but this is not without its reasons. First, my own limited education and lack of experience at the time left them in need of mature development. Second, the sketches were written without any model to look to for guidance; they are entirely the creation of my own imagination. Third, because the sketches were written for a magazine, they are intentionally brief. Recalling my motivation for writing these sketches takes me back to the austere circumstances I was in when I started writing them. I often give an empathetic sigh for the young monks of my generation because of what we had to endure during our first years in Taiwan!

I remember the time when I began writing the first paragraph of my first sketch. It was after my abbot had asked me to help him by guarding a dense forest. A monastic, like anyone else, cannot live without the basic necessities of food and shelter, so during those uncertain vagabond days, I had to bow to circumstances for three meals a day and a place to live. To meet the basic necessities of life, I began selling my youthful vigor as cheap labor.

During those days, I would trek up and down the mountain, going to and fro through the jungle; I was like a hunter myself—always keeping a watchful eye for any movement on the mountain. The poachers' targets were the boar, wildcats, deer, and hare. My responsibility was to make sure they did not also steal any timber. By daytime, I would watch the macaques and squirrels scurrying nimbly through the dense vegetation, and I would calculate the time for the arrival of my meals that were brought from the temple. Deep in the night, alone, as I lay on my mat in a tiny thatched hut on the mountainside, I would listen to the screech of the owls and the whistling of the wind through the branches of the pine and cedar trees. This labor—apart from food, shelter and altruistic satisfaction—came with no remuneration. So, as time went by, I started to sense the unstoppable ticking of time and fear that my youth was slipping away. Which youth is not filled with eagerness and enthusiasm? Which young person does not ponder the future with a hopeful heart? I thought that I should not let my valuable youth pass by in this meaningless way. I wanted to leave some mark of my life's journey behind. That is why, in that thatched hut, barely large enough for one person, I lay on the wild-grass-covered floor of the hut and began to write the first sketch about the big bell.

I remember once having a casual conversation with Master Xinwu (心悟). He had said, "The current ability of the intellectual skills of exploration, investigation, and research of Chinese people is far less developed compared to the ability of those in other countries. The wisdom of young Buddhists today compared to ancient times is also somewhat less profound." His words were true indeed! But where did the heart of the problem lie? Other countries had so many outstanding scholars. *Why was this?* I wondered. I realized it was because those countries had educational policies that supported and directly facilitated advanced scholarship and research. If a person was interested in a particular area of knowledge and willing to specialize and do research in that field, then all living and research expenses were paid by the government. Even if the research lasted for decades, that scholar or researcher would be supported because those governments wanted them to be able to focus on their work. I think that if you study something for decades, then, even if you are not an expert from the start, you will certainly become one!

In my formidable homeland of China, the government has long considered education to be a person's own responsibility that, essentially, has nothing to do with the nation itself. Consequently, few experts emerge. It has been the same with the Buddhist religion. Taking refuge in Buddhism, young Buddhists would leave their families and, already suffering from an inadequate education, would still lack access to systematic teachings from a master. One hand would be flipping books and the other hand longing for enough paper, ink, and brush-pens. Aside from buying a couple of books when you had some money, there were no Buddhist libraries for finding information. In this situation, one can place no blame on the young Buddhists of those days for their lack of wisdom.

In addition, living under the authority of abbots and the senior monks who only expected you to haul wood, carry water, and sweep the floor did not lend itself to learning. At best they would allow you to split your time between work and study. Furthermore, the lay people, not knowing any better, only expected the monks to chant and make prostrations to the Buddha. If they saw you reading the Tripitaka, with its twelve canonical divisions, they would criticize you for not practicing properly, but if they heard your fingers hastening over the Buddhist prayer beads, they called you a proper and ethical monastic. As a result, young Buddhist monks did whatever pleased the laity. How was a young Buddhist monk supposed to gain deeper wisdom?

While writing these sketches, I received much encouragement, which was very exciting, but at the same time, I also heard some well-intended criticism. The eighth sketch, "Censer," concludes with a scene of one young Buddhist making his own ten sincere vows. Because of the content of his vows, waves of opposing voices came at me from people whom I could only view as simply recalcitrant and disingenuous.

These people said that Buddhists should not place curses on people who have died. Some even claimed that the sketch itself revealed to outsiders too much of Buddhism's "dirty laundry". I do agree that Buddhists should not place curses on the dead. Like the arhat, even if someone were to come at him with a knife, the arhat would simply show where to cut his neck; he does not strike back. But if a situation involved the protection of a sentient being, a Mahayana bodhisattva would pick up a knife and kill the demons so that sentient beings could live safely and peacefully.

These fictional sketches are not intended to be read solely on a literal level. Chinese literary style does not require these sketches to be solemn in order to be edifying. Like Japanese *monogatari* poetry, they are meant to be literary and artistic creations, and the significance of literary writing lies in its ability to reflect reality, to praise what is good, and to point out what is bad.

A person who has an affinity for literature is first and foremost an independent person. He must use his own mind for independent thought; he must use his own eyes for observation; and he must use his own powers of reasoning! If not, he is nothing more than a parrot or a tape recorder! Literature does not speak for only one person; it speaks for everyone. Even when speaking on behalf of religion, rather than have the attitude of a scholar, it is better to speak with kindness and gentleness. When it comes to Buddhism, save for those followers who have become calloused and numb, what person with ambition and enthusiasm would not feel this way?

The value of literature for young Buddhists lies in its courageous expression, not in its being an impediment placed by elderly monks. Don't be overly suspicious! I may be causing myself verbal karmic effects, but damn those people. Even if I suffer misfortune, as long as Buddhism flourishes, I will be happy to accept the effects.

The meanings of words can be understood differently by different readers. I heard one venerable giving a talk in which he especially pointed out the ten great vows and gave an explanation of them, praising how my book is full of enthusiastic devotion to Buddhism. I know that most Buddhist practitioners are understanding people; however, I don't wish to create afflictions over my book. This is why I have made some slight changes to this sketch.

At that time, the editor-in-chief of *Awakening Life* magazine was also the main editor of the periodical *Bodhi Tree.* Thankfully, he was an open-minded person, or else the life of my Dharma instruments and items would have come to an end at that time. This attitude that the sketches revealed too much behind-the-scenes information about Buddhism and that they should not be published puzzled me greatly. The Buddhist teachings are not political, and there is no so called behind-the-scenes. True followers of the Buddhist religion worry about people not knowing *enough* about the teachings and they work to promote knowledge of Buddhism. My initial vow in writing these sketches was to help people better understand what Buddhism is and what it is not. The differences between righteousness and evil, good and bad, right and wrong—we must make the Buddhist teachings clear!

While I was writing the sketches, many people thought that I was intentionally trying to embarrass them. The people whom I described in the "donation record" sketch thought I was directing the story at them. The chanting repentance sutra monastics also thought the words I wrote were deliberately aimed at them. Regarding this, I can only say that sometimes people are way too sensitive!

In my sketches, I refrained from revealing the true identities of who said or did what, but the stories I wrote, the things that happened, and the words I used did, indeed, occur in real life. Collecting alms for the public welfare is not a bad thing, but collecting alms solely for the good of an individual is selfish. Sutra chanting can be done; one just needs to follow according to the law of the Dharma or it really brings shame to Buddhism. Buddhists of today ought to make these problems known, and lay our cards on the table. Buddhism has become an enterprise, and people use the name of Buddhism to make a living. People depend upon the Buddha to stay alive, and they actually try to "sell" the Buddha. This is truly disheartening!

I wrote these sketches in hopes of severing the harmful practices of Buddhist followers, but I know this is much to wish for. But I have learned that many people upon reading these sketches have gained a clearer understanding of the right and wrong way to practice Buddhism! Many have even realized an affinity with Buddhism and become Buddhists!

Now, my sketches are being published together under the title *Bells, Gongs, and Wooden Fish: Voices for Buddhist Change,* but the ordinary items that are a part of the daily life of a Chinese Buddhist temple are not limited to just these twenty. It is my hope that, in the near future, I can add ten or twenty more sketches. I would wish to make the sketches more concise and to create an example for all the teachings of the Buddha. I hope readers will offer me some suggestions.

Hsing Yun
Taipei, 1953

Big Bell

I am Big Bell
forever hanging high in the temple.
I send forth my robust voice
to awaken those indulgent ones.
Let everyone for themselves and
others establish the banner of
Buddhism. May it flourish and
fly freely in the sky.

In temples and monasteries, the big bell is struck to announce the time and gather the assembly. Except for the ceramic bells of earliest times, temple bells are cast from copper or iron and are shaped like an over-turned cup. The surface of the bell is decorated simply, and the lip is even and round. The bell has a loop at the top so that it can be suspended from a bell tower.

Bells in China have long been used in ceremonies and musical performances, before being incorporated into Buddhism. Major Dharma services and offerings all use the bell to accompany chanting. The bell is rung to show the solemnity of the occasion to all attending, but is also used to show a warm welcome for visiting senior monastics or dignitaries.

The ringing of the bell is a reminder to practitioners that they must strike with diligent effort to beat away the afflictions that have accumulated since beginningless time. Those who strike the bell should also make a compassionate vow that the sound of the bell resonate all the way to heaven and can penetrate all the way to hell, so that all those beings who hear the bell can awaken to the wisdom of intrinsic nature and attain peace.

I am called Big Bell. From olden times until the present, I have been hanging high up in a corner of the Great Hall of this temple. Not long ago, there was a monastic standing beside me holding a copy of an American magazine with a picture of another bell on it. I was filled with joy to see this great, big bell, as there is only one of us in each temple, and sometimes I get quite lonely. When I saw the picture of that friend, I could hardly contain my happiness. I gave that bell such a warm smile. Oh, then I recognized it! It was the Liberty Bell of America!

The Liberty Bell, as you may recall, was the one whose brave voice chimed out at the first public reading of the American colonists' Declaration of Independence. Later, in 1835, it was reportedly cracked when knelled at the funeral of John Marshall, the thirteenth chief justice of the United States Supreme Court. Today it still bears the honorable scars as a memento of those historic occasions, as it hangs near Independence Hall in Philadelphia for all to revere. As I think about some important events in my own past, I realize that we both are bells of freedom! I cannot help but think about my own life and swell with boundless emotion.

As the big bell here in this serene temple, I am different from all the other Dharma instruments. My large, heavy body may keep me stationary, but no obstacle is able to block my great voice. My ring carries through curtains, over rooftops and mountains, and resounds freely through the air. That is why people also call *me* a "symbol of freedom."

I use my voice sparingly, though, never sounding without good cause. Usually singing out twice a day, I am up bright and early in the morning without delay to ring in a new dawn, and during the silence of the night, someone will come to strike me announcing the time for rest. When I toll at night with my voice resounding solemnly through the darkness, people say I am the "signal for slumber." Numerous sentient beings take their repose when they hear my voice, and I awaken them when the sun is rising. I not only announce the beginning and ending of every day but also sound the alarm for everyone to gather for an important event or in the case of an emergency. My duty is a grand and glorious one!

There is one elder monastic who is my best friend. Whenever he comes to ring me, whether morning or night, he always accompanies me with the "Gatha of the Bell." He sings one line of his *gatha* following each of my notes. His robust, yet plaintive voice joins with mine, arousing mindfulness in all who hear our heartfelt harmony and transporting listeners to a realm of peace. The elder monastic's song goes like this:

> When the mighty bell was first rung,
> > the gatha was sung.
> It reached up to the skies and down to hell.
> May wars cease, as soldiers and galloping
> > war horses stop fighting.
> May those who were defeated and killed be
> > reborn in the Pure Land.
> May all beings in the three realms be freed
> > from the cycle of birth and death.
> May all beings be liberated from the
> > sea of suffering.

My friend's deep compassion resounds in the sincere words of his song. In addition to my friend, many poets have celebrated my existence, especially Zhang Ji, a well-known poet of the Tang dynasty, who wrote a famous poem about me. I'll recite it for you:

> Moon sets, crows caw,
> > sky is full of frost;
> River maples, fishing-boat lights
> > break through my troubled sleep.
> Beyond the city of Suzhou lies
> > Han Shan monastery.
> At midnight the clang of the bell
> > reaches the traveler's boat.

My voice is heard at midnight across the land, touching the hearts of those who are miles away. Upon hearing my sound, travelers far from their homes pause with longing and a heightened sense of life's vicissitudes. I also awaken the travelers from their dreams. The young, renewed with great vigor when they hear my voice, put any hardship and injustice behind them and valiantly press on toward their goals.

Do you need more evidence? Which monastic in the temple, upon awakening to my voice, has not hurried to continue their practice and be liberated from the suffering of birth and death? Which resident living near the temple, upon hearing my voice, has not been encouraged to get up and get ready for the day? When my voice resounds—reaching villages, cities, fields, and mountains—it becomes a light in the darkness, reminding everyone to be mindful of the impermanence and temporariness of life.

I remember one time when a friendly visitor came to the temple and passed by me saying, "Oh, Bell! I love your deep and lingering vibrations. Every time I hear you it's like a familiar call, wafting from a Buddha land. Why don't you just make one big clang, and knock awake those people who are living lives of self indulgence!"

I remember another time when a young monastic, full of unexpressed emotions, passed by me. "Oh, Bell," he said. "I'm so fond of your smoothly disseminating voice. It resonates so deeply and carries over such a long distance. I can't even count the number of ignorant people in whom you have awakened the urge to pursue the true meaning of life. Buddhism is declining, and since many Buddhists are as if dreaming in a deep sleep, why don't you make one big clang, knock them all awake, and revive people's interest in the Buddha's path?"

The countless numbers who have prayed near me and lingered within the reaches of my voice have wished that my sonorous tone be shot up to the clouds in the sky—reaching the inner depths of the self-indulgent and calling them out of their lives of delusion.

I do not want to keep silent. I am usually eager to sing out. But I have been misused by people; allow me to recall one such occasion. A famous, wealthy person had come to the temple on a casual visit. As he was leaving, the abbot of the temple asked one of the monks to strike me so that my voice could be used as a spectacular farewell to this visitor. While I was ringing, another monk with a stern face came up to me. "Apple polisher!" he called me. "You green bell! Pandering to money!" he scolded. "You are forsaking the honor and importance of your duty! Your responsibility is to awaken ignorant people and to wake up the monastics in the morning."

Well, the words of that monk resonated to my iron core. Every word he said was right; I do have a pure and noble calling. I hope that abbots will never use me so unethically again. After this ordeal, I resolved to use my voice to bring hope to the despondent and to make the hearts of the courageous even stronger. *Bong! Bong! Bong!* Listen! I am singing with all my might! I want to use my fierce roar to sing!

> I am Big Bell
>> forever hanging high in the temple.
> I send forth my robust voice
>> to awaken those indulgent ones.
> Let everyone for themselves and others
>> establish the banner of Buddhism.
> May it flourish and fly freely in the sky.

Great Gong

I am known as King of the Dharma Instruments, it is my destiny to lead, as everyone listens for my voice to know when to start and stop chanting, when to chant quickly or slowly, and when to change from one tone to another.

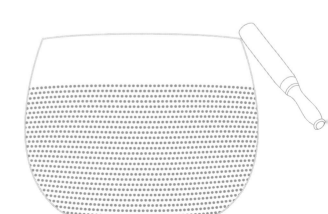

The great gong can be found in Buddhist temples usually to the right of the main altar. Ranging from thirty to sixty centimeters in diameter, great gongs are bowl-shaped and cast from copper. The gong is struck by the discipline master during Dharma services at the beginning to set the pace and the pitch of the chanting, and at the conclusion of the service to signal its end. The gong is also struck whenever senior monastics, great sages, or visiting abbots come to the temple and bow in the main shrine, one strike for each bow, as a respectful welcome.

Sometimes called a chime, the instrument comes in many shapes and sizes: large chimes, round chimes, tablet chimes, and handheld chimes. Tablet chimes, for example, are made of stone and shaped similar to the cloud board used to signal meals. The tablet chime is hung in the corridor leading to the abbot's chambers, and it is sounded three times by the receptionist when a visitor is to see the abbot. The handheld chime, also called a hand bell, is shaped like a small bowl and is attached to a wooden handle by a knot through a hole in its center. The hand bell is struck with a small steel rod when bowing to the Buddha and chanting to indicate when to start or stop.

I do not recall in which year we great gongs first came to Buddhist temples in China. I think it might have been after Chan Master Mazu Daoyi had founded his monastery and Chan Master Baizhang Huaihai had established the monastic rules. I was then enlisted for my honorable duty.

I come from a long pedigree of the Brass family, but there are other distinguished alloys in my ancestry as well. I am known as King of the Dharma Instruments, but it is said that I am actually akin to the small hand chime, another one of the wondrous Dharma instruments in the monastery. It is my destiny to lead, as everyone listens for my voice to know when to start and stop chanting, when to chant quickly or slowly, and when to change from one tone to another. I live in the Great Hall of this temple. My place is right in front of all the other Dharma instruments. I feel most fortunate because my life is good and I have a fulfilling purpose.

Let me tell you about my contribution to my calling. When I sound one *dong*, the instruments follow my lead and start playing. When I sound two *dongs*, the instruments stop. I am like a bugle's call in the military, telling the soldiers when to advance and when to retreat. I take great pride in my role. When I sound my voice, I must be right on cue. There is no room for dereliction of duty in my position. Just as if the bugle were to make a mistake, then the soldiers would become disorderly; it is the same in my case. If I were to err, then all the other instruments and the Buddhist practitioners would most certainly fall out of step. The chanters could not keep their cadence in unison. Everything would quickly fall into a terrible discordant cacophony. Therefore, you can see what an honorable and important office I discharge.

A great gong is different from the other Dharma instruments in another way. Any one of the monastics can strike them, but such is not the case with me. The monastic who strikes me has a special title: chant leader. The chant leader is an important administrator in the monastery who is not only required to be familiar with temple etiquette but must also possess a superior vocal quality for chanting. Just as in a traditional Chinese opera, the actor in the leading role has to direct the performance, so it is with the chant leader during a Dharma service. There is a very specific technique to use when striking a great gong, and the chant leader must not make a careless mistake. Next to the chant leader's meditation cushion in the meditation hall is a small wooden plaque on which the following grave admonition is inscribed:

> A practitioner's life of wisdom
>   relies on you fulfilling your office properly.
> If you perform your duty carelessly,
>   you shall bear that wrongdoing.

As you can see, striking the great gong is not a small, insignificant task.

The chant leader's position has always been an important and responsible one because of the great gong's critical role in the Dharma service. Many envy that position, claiming that the chant leader simply likes to show off. Some monastics erroneously believe that they would gain honor and importantness if they only had the opportunity to strike me. Thus, I have, at times, been the object of the struggle for power. I have often been exploited by the

monastics who have selfish reasons for being appointed to strike me. These monastics will typically be the only ones competing for the position of chant leader, because, in general, the more mature cultivators have no interest in engaging in such petty rivalries.

I have already called your attention to the fact that I am the leader of the other Dharma instruments used for chanting. As a rule, people are not allowed to arbitrarily strike me. However, in the past, elderly, superstitious women would come to the temple and cry, "If I come to offer incense but don't strike the great gong, then the bodhisattvas will not believe that I'm sincere." Then with little regard, they would march right up and start pounding on me. Bang! Bang! Clang! Clang! The master in charge of the Great Hall would be at a loss for words. Personally, I entertained these misguided actions as only a mild disturbance, and I secretly laughed at the naiveté of the elderly women. I am sure that the bodhisattvas care more about the sincerity of one's intentions when offering incense, rather than whether or not one has struck a great gong.

During times of peace in the land, my life has been very stable. But, unfortunately, during times of war, I have suffered greatly. There have been three disastrous times of persecution in the history of Chinese Buddhism. We refer to these as the Four Scourges of Buddhism[1]. Emperor Zhou Shizong only saw me as an object of valuable metal, and he ordered that all brass bells like me be collected and stamped into imperial currency. When I heard about this plan, I was terrified! I believed my life was doomed! Fortunately for me, Emperor Zhou's rule lasted only a few years before he was overthrown. My life was spared, and a safe existence was assured for me.

Many centuries passed in this way. Then the Luguo Bridge Incident[2] happened. On July 7, 1937, my homeland was invaded by the Japanese army. The many monastics who did not wish to live under Japanese rule followed the Chinese government as it retreated to the unoccupied areas. The monastics carried many valuable Buddhist treasures with them, but my great weight caused them to leave me behind. I remained in the occupied territory, and I was destined to bear another long period of hardship.

After eight years of occupation, the Japanese army was running short of guns and ammunition. In their desperation, the soldiers turned to me, thinking that my body could be smelted into guns and bullets. Hearing the soldiers telling the monastics about their plans was like a bolt of lightning striking me! I thought that my fate had been sealed, and that, this time, I was most certainly finished!

Fortunately, the monastics did not want me destroyed. They came up with a clever plan to hide me in the corner of one of the rooms in the temple. There I would be concealed from the view of the Japanese soldiers. A monastic told the soldiers that the monastery had been without a great gong for many years, and offered to show them around to see for themselves.

As luck would have it, the Japanese soldiers failed to find my hiding place, so they had to abandon their plans. I remained in my dark hiding place for eight years, patiently waiting to be rescued—steadfastly waiting for victory and freedom. Finally, the war ended. There was peace. Once again, I proudly took my place at the center of the Great Hall.

After this ordeal, I made a bold statement: All who want to destroy me will end up only destroying themselves. I am a Dharma instrument, dedicated to only being used during Dharma services. The "eyes and ears" of heavenly beings can never be destroyed by mere mortals.

Unfortunately, disaster, like a bad penny, turned up again. A civil war broke out, and Buddhism was in great danger. After all that had happened throughout my long history, I decided that the place of my birth was no longer safe for me. I did not want to live another eight years shrouded in darkness, so I traveled by ship over the ocean to Taiwan. When I arrived, I wandered around like a vagabond. Once again, hard times had found me. I was certain that my days of glory were forever in the past!

In my initial days here in Taiwan, I was not treated with the dignity and respect that had finally been accorded me in my home-land. While in China—with the exception of those naïve old ladies who insisted on striking me when they offered incense—only the trained chant leader would strike me. But in Taiwan, anyone could hit me! Mr. Li struck me. Mr. Zhang beat me. Numerous monas-tics hit me. Laypeople pounded on me. Furthermore, the people here did not know the proper technique when striking me, so my rhythm was shamefully uneven and my tone terribly discordant. The inexperienced monastics occasionally made mistakes and dis-tracted the chant leader. When that happened, the two would ex-change uneasy glances. These distractions would make the chanters lose their concentration. Consequently, I could tell that their minds wandered off to other thoughts, detracting from their cultivation.

There was one other difference in the way I was treated. In China, the chanting always started with the chant leader striking me. In Taiwan, sometimes the chant leader would begin by striking me, but sometimes before he started to intone the chant, the pre-siding monastic would also jump in, throwing him off and causing discord. By the time the chant leader was back on track, many striking cues had already been missed. What can I say about this improper situation?

What distressed me even more was when the abbot would take me along for funeral services and other rituals. This was a very disheartening experience, because the chanting ceremonies in Taiwan included words, rites, and even memorial tablets of folk religions or other traditions, rather than following traditional Buddhist ritual.

I wondered about what would happen to me. Since I had been exposed in public as a party to these unorthodox practices, if I ever returned to my homeland, how could I face my fellow Dharma instruments? Thank goodness that some compassionate followers of the Buddha did not allow my life to continue to go down such a path. They came to my rescue and installed me in my current place of honor—the glorious Great Hall of this wonderful temple, where I am, once again, King of the Dharma Instruments.

Photograph by Ven. Hui Rong

Wooden Fish

*I'm treated with the
utmost respect every day.
When the monastics use me for
chanting, they hold me in front of
their hearts. When they are not
using me, they carefully place me
near the statues of the Buddhas.
They act just like I'm the "eyes
and ears" of heavenly beings.*

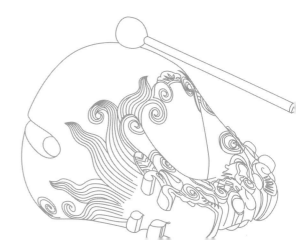

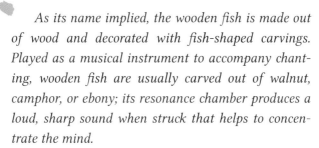

As its name implied, the wooden fish is made out of wood and decorated with fish-shaped carvings. Played as a musical instrument to accompany chanting, wooden fish are usually carved out of walnut, camphor, or ebony; its resonance chamber produces a loud, sharp sound when struck that helps to concentrate the mind.

During chanting sessions the sound of the wooden fish invigorates the listeners with its rhythm, helping the chanters to overcome drowsiness and distraction and enriching the music of the service for the audience. Chanters should strike the wooden fish in accordance with the middle way: neither too fast nor too slow, just as mindfulness should not be too tense nor too lax.

Striking the wooden fish should remind the practitioner of the fish's special talent: whether swimming or remaining still, a fish's eyes are always open. In the same way, the wooden fish urges us to be diligent and work hard.

M any years ago, I was part of an evergreen tree living in a forest on the very top of a high mountain. One day, a woodcutter hiked up to the top of the mountain, chopped down the tree, and took it to a shop where Buddhist supplies were made. There my destiny was in the hands of a woodcarver who changed my life by making me into a "wooden fish." A few days later, someone clad in what I recognized as a Chinese monastic robe came into the shop and bought me. I don't know how much he gave for me, but he took me to live in the majestic Great Hall of a temple. A drum, a great gong, and a small hand chime became my best friends.

All year long, I am able to keep myself alert, for I never need a wink of sleep. I'm fashioned to have a strong and cadent voice. They say it's quite unique—like the sound of the rushing currents of the Yangzi River and the roaring tide of the Pacific Ocean. My percussive timbre—keeping time with the gently rolling, melodic chanting of the monastics—contributes greatly to the sanctity of Dharma services. Whether I am leading a gathering of tens, hundreds, or even thousands, everyone follows my tempo. Each time I am struck, voices rise—united and harmonious. Even those outside of the Great Hall who hear my voice become solemn and respectful.

One day, a guest who was temporarily living in the temple passed by me. He was talking with another visitor saying, "This morning around five o'clock, through my open window, I heard the sound of a bell, and then I heard the monastics chanting to the beat of the wooden fish. I felt as if carried to a pure land—so peaceful—as if all human worries had been washed away. I was touched so deeply by this experience that I now appreciate the traditional Dharma instruments more than the modern ones." When I heard this, I realized how much meaning I brought to the lives of others. I was overcome with a sense of purpose for my life.

Since loving-kindness and compassion are important in Buddhism, some people may wonder why during chanting the monastics strike something that looks like a fish. Well, it's for the simple reason that fish never close their eyes. The wooden fish is used as a symbol to remind everybody to stay "awake" and pay attention to their cultivation. I'm treated with the utmost respect every day. When the monastics use me for chanting, they hold me in front of their hearts. When they are not using me, they carefully place me near the statues of the Buddhas. They act just like I'm the "eyes and ears" of heavenly beings. They never hit me purposelessly. I sure enjoy my place in life and hope I'll always live right here in the Great Hall.

Another time, something quite unexpected occurred. Some students from the National Music Academy in Nanjing who knew Chinese music and had been influenced by Buddhist chanting came to the temple. They were studying Buddhist music. They had tried using modern instruments, but they didn't like the result. The students were here to ask the abbot about borrowing my friends and me for their music. The musicians were lavish in their praise of Buddhist music—expressing their appreciation for the influence of Buddhist music on the overall development of Chinese music. They specifically praised me for my special contribution as a musical instrument. Boy, when I heard this, I could've jumped for joy. I smiled proudly at those modern instruments!

A Chinese proverb goes something like this: "The flower's bloom is fleeting; dazzling scenes are ephemeral." This sure is true, for dark days awaited me. It all began when the monastery where I was living at the time wanted to build a dormitory for the monastics but they were just a bit short on funds. One day the abbot came carrying a yellow cloth shoulder bag. He gathered me up and took me into town with him to ask for donations. He started striking me and loudly reciting "NA-MO A-MI-TO FO."[3] In this way, he hoped to receive donations from passersby. But some people didn't appreciate the abbot's sincere efforts to promote the Triple Gem in this way. They belittled our efforts, and gruffly dismissed us as being incapable of caring for ourselves without begging for alms. Buddhism was being tarnished by us. As the abbot struck me day after day, the scoffing and ridicule became louder and stronger. People seemed to be losing their respect for me, and I started to question the worth of my life.

Another saying warns that misfortune comes in threes. And sure enough, I was about to be handed number two. It was when we were at another village seeking donations that my poor abbot became ill. He passed away right then and there, leaving me all alone. I didn't know what to do; I felt just like an orphan. That's when a raggedy, unscrupulous beggar saw that I was there all by myself, and he grabbed me up. He started going around pretending to be a monk. He would beat on me every day to get people's attention, and then he would beg for food and money. When people didn't give him any money, he would just get angrier and whack me even harder. My voice became so harsh that people started hating me.

Those who had some knowledge of Buddhism didn't blame me for being misused by the abbot in that a way. But the average person couldn't tell the difference between the real monastics and the deceptive beggars. At that time, as more beggars pretended to be monks—by hitting us wooden fish and asking for alms—both monks *and* beggars came to be equally distrusted. It didn't matter to me that my own life was in the hands of a beggar, but when I saw the real monastics being disparaged like that, I felt so sorry and ashamed for them.

Later, the beggar who had been abusing me came into some money, and, no doubt, desiring to move on to a new scheme, sold me to a performing troupe. The entertainers were putting on a play at a famous theater in Shanghai. The play was called *Eighteen Arhats Defeat the Giant Roc Bird.* Every single one of the eighteen men who played the roles of the *arhats* had a wooden fish. In the play, when the giant bird attacked the *arhats* with its sword-like wings, they used me as a weapon to fend off the bird. I was so afraid! I thought that I was going to die! During that time, who could have known how sad I felt?

I was also forced to be in another play called *Shixu Seeks Pleasure on Green Screen Mountain.* I was shamelessly used as the signal that it was safe for a man to have a secret rendezvous with a woman. One day, two monks saw the play. Naturally, they were outraged. Now I ask you, who believes that I would willingly play such a part? One of the monks said with tears streaming down his face, "No wonder Buddhism has declined. We live in sad times with so many people trying to destroy Buddhism. It is most painful to see such a dedicated Dharma instrument being misused. This play caters to the baser instincts of the ordinary townspeople and misrepresents Buddhism. Why aren't the monasteries here doing something to protect the Dharma instruments from being desecrated in this way?"

Then there were the Buddhist zealots who saw us wooden fish being used in these strange ways and urged that we all be rounded up and burned! I was pretty nervous when I heard this. I was tired of being mistreated in this world, and I longed to escape from those people and get back to the Great Hall of my monastery. Cutting me into little pieces for firewood was going way too far, because *I* wasn't the problem. It was those people who were misusing me. That's when I decided to raise my own voice to all the compassionate followers of the Buddha pleading, "In order to reform Buddhism, please rescue me soon!"

Censer

My life has been blessed with good fortune. People have always praised me, especially during Dharma services. The words "noble" and "graceful" have been used to describe me in songs.
Don't underestimate me.
I might be just an ordinary object, but I have an extraordinarily great responsibility.

Censers are commonly placed on the altar table, and are for burning incense as an offering to the Buddha. When a censer is joined with vases for flowers and with candleholders they form a set called "the three essentials." When a stick of incense is offered in a censer it forms a connection between the human mind and the Buddha's mind. The main purpose of an incense burner is to provide a container for offering burnt incense, but they can also serve to enhance the dignity of a room or hall. The continuous burning of incense reflects the bodhisattva's continuity of mindfulness and spirit of diligent effort.

Censers may be made from metals such as gold, silver, copper, nickel, and bronze, as well as clay, ceramic, ivory, and sandalwood. There are three main types of censers: tabletop, portable, and standing. Tabletop censers may be bowl-shaped for holding spiral incense, or may be built to hold a single stick vertically or horizontally. Portable or "handheld" censers are small censers with handles that are usually used during welcoming ceremonies. Standing censers have three legs and sit on the ground, and may or may not have handles. The type of incense and the method of offering it varies depending on the type of censer being used.

Photograph by Ven. Hui Rong

E veryone knows who *I* am. When my name comes up, there isn't a person who hasn't heard of me before. I'm such a popular Dharma object that I'm not just confined to monasteries or temples. I'm also a household item. Even children know me. People often display me in conspicuous places in their living rooms. I'm crafted from porcelain, ceramic, copper, or tin, and my body is decorated with many different kinds of patterns, sometimes even with the names of temples.

When my name is mentioned, people associate me with the burning of incense. I'm the one used for offering incense to the Buddha, and I couldn't be left out of the offering services for honoring ancestors. During memorial services, when it comes time for the incense offering, there will be absolute silence and everyone will be quiet and solemn. No one will say a word until all of the incense has been placed in my burner.

My life has been blessed with good fortune. People have always praised me, especially during Dharma services. The words "noble" and "graceful" have been used to describe me in songs. Here are a couple of lines from the offering verse, *In Praise of Incense*: "Incense now is burning in the censer / Fragrance permeates the dharma realm." When you see the flower-shaped cloud of incense rising from me, it makes you feel just like you're being transported to the heaven realm. What could be as sublimely beautiful as this?

During Dharma services, the presiding monastic walks to the front of the altar, kneels down in front of me, faces the statue of the Buddha, and offers three sticks of incense. He's actually using me to show his sincerity. I'm honored to be a bridge between the human world and the Buddha. Don't underestimate me. I might be just an ordinary object, but I have an extraordinarily great responsibility. For centuries in China incense, flowers, lamps, perfume, fruit, tea, food, treasure, beads, and cloth have been the traditional ten offerings made to the Buddha. Since incense is always the first one named, naturally I'm first-string among the offerings. Some people buy very expensive incense to burn in me. There are many types of incense and a wide variety of fragrances. Sandalwood is my brand.

The fragrance of incense is unique from all other aromas. A lot of people, whether they are Buddhists or not, have an incense burner and some first-rate incense. Can you believe it? Some people don't burn incense to the Buddha! They just indulge in it for their own pleasure! When I see this, it's like these people are just taking advantage of the fragrance we censers provide.

A long time ago in China, scholars who had failed their imperial, civil service examinations passed the time by writing stories that began with a seven-character poem. The first line of the poem would always have a reference to me. Here's an example of one: "Incense burns in the purple and gold censer / I come from Luoyang." Seems like those schoolboys back then couldn't write anything without starting out mentioning me. In those days, my reputation and influence were fabled across the land.

When I'm warming the bench, I like to people watch. I keep my eyes on the gestures and expressions of the devotees, and I've made some observations. The ones who have been Buddhists for years know to use their left hand when they put their incense sticks in my burner. I can see that the people who use their right hand

大雄寶殿
Da Xiong Bao Dian

Photographs by Ven. Hui Rong

don't understand Buddhist rituals very much. It's taught that the devotee's right hand is, in many cases, the hand that creates a person's karma, while the left hand doesn't. This is why people use their left hand to offer incense.

Buddhists show their respect to Buddhas and bodhisattvas by offering incense in hopes of reducing their suffering and attaining enlightenment. But I don't think some people really understand the reason for offering incense, because all they do is petition for health and wealth. They even make requests for favors, such as having sons or good marriages. There's a little folk tune about this practice. I'll sing it for you.

> Shrine of the city god!
> Grand is your hall!
> So many come to light incense for you.
> Some place the sticks,
> for wealth do they pray.
> Why does the maiden light incense today?

> Shrine of the city god!
> Grand is your hall!
> So many come to light incense for you!
> Married maid asks good luck for her son.
> Young maiden burns to find the right one.

The practice of offering incense has a long history in Buddhism. Not only have people never wanted to get rid of me, like what has happened to some of my Dharma instrument friends, but many educated people have been my advocate. Dr. Hu Shezi, a well-known scholar and writer, urged the abolition of burning paper money during funerals. In his article, "Funeral Revolution," he proposed that people should pay their respects to the deceased by using incense. People liked Dr. Hu's idea, and since the offering of incense was accepted by people, I didn't have to worry about my future. Thank you, Buddha!

In the past, at funeral services and other Dharma ceremonies, the presiding monastic would ask the sponsor of the ceremony to kneel down behind him and raise a small censer. I think this was done because, at that time, most people who sponsored the Dharma ceremonies didn't know how to chant sutras themselves and would become uncomfortable from kneeling for long periods. By having the sponsors participate in the ceremony, the monastics showed generosity and sympathy toward them.

I've witnessed some strange things, which I can only laugh about. On one occasion, two men were having a terrible quarrel. No one could get them to make up. Finally, each man bought a bundle of incense sticks. They each placed their sticks in me, knelt down, and made their vows. The one said, "With Buddha as my witness, if I, Zhang San have stolen Lee Si's money, may I take sick and die suddenly." The other one said, "If I, Lee Si, have falsely accused Zhang San, may I not have a natural, peaceful death." Their actions puzzled me, for only they knew who was right and who was wrong. Buddha and I were not the ones to judge them.

Sick people will come to burn incense, too. There was a time when they would wrap the ashes in paper and take them home to use as medicine that they believed would cure their ills. Other foolish people copied this example and started wrapping ashes in little yellow pieces of paper. They brought them to the Great Hall by the thousands! They would offer them, chanting "*om mani padme hum*,"⁴ believing that the use of the mantra and the ashes would be a powerful medicine to cure all diseases. To think that a hallowed temple had been used as an herbal medicine shop!

This was a time when the Dharma was weak. Few people came to offer incense in the temple where I lived. Unfortunately, many pilgrims went instead to shrines of the city god and shrines of the sea goddess. I didn't care if people admired me or not, but I did want people to know the teachings of the Buddha. I wanted them to avoid those foolish practices that were harmful. If the harm of such superstitious practices was not ended, how would the Dharma ever prosper? I prayed that the wise and compassionate followers of the Buddha would become aware of this dangerous situation and do something about it.

I see that most people these days come to offer incense to the Buddha to pray, make vows, and repent. I get all choked up when I see the sincerity and determination of their hearts. I remember one time when a young Buddhist came and placed three sticks of incense in my burner early one morning. He knelt before me, faced the Buddha, and made ten vows. Who except for me would ever know his deep feelings of grief at that time? After making his vows, tears ran down his cheeks. I prayed for him asking that he would be able to fulfill his vows. These are the vows he made:

One
May all sentient beings in the universe
leave the sea of suffering!

Two
May virtuous monks live long lives and
the Dharma continue in the Saha world!

Three
May every civil and military official
in the land support Buddhism!

Four
May the Seven Classes of Disciples
of the Triple Gem be united for the sake
of the Dharma and all sentient beings!

Five
May all parents, enemies, and relatives
from all lives be liberated to
the Pure Land instantly
by the Buddha's radiance!

Six
May the conservative elders be able to
keep pace with the times and
create more Dharma activities!

Seven
May all the misguided laymen and
laywomen soon repent and
not fall into the hell realm!

Eight
May ambitious young Buddhists and
the eminent monastics who teach the
Dharma let go of the conflicts between
them and modernize Buddhism!

Nine
May all outside religions abandon
the darkness and move towards the light!

Ten
May the monks who put on western-style
clothing and the nuns who don't shave
their heads still be sangha gems and
not bad examples for Buddhism!

By the time this young man had finished his ten vows, tears were streaming down his cheeks. I also said a prayer, wishing that all his vows would come true.

Cushion

*We cushions have
never been limited to only
Buddhist monasteries and temples;
we are found in many places.
Every family—rich or poor,
prominent or humble,
large or small—
makes use of us cushions.*

Round and flat and traditionally woven from rush grass, a prayer cushion is used in a shrine room while meditating or kneeling so as not to soil one's clothing. There is a rich variety of prayer cushions: some are thick and round, some are woven from lyon's grass, while some are even ring-shaped with holes in the middle.

Prayer cushions also vary widely through the various regions of China due to differences in climate, geography, and local custom. Some cushions are round and made of cloth, while others are low stools made solely from wood.

The prayer cushion assists practitioners in making a mind-to-mind connection with the Buddha, for it is with the cushion that we bow to the Buddha and seek repentance. When bowing, we devoutly express our admiration and deep regard for the Buddha. We can also seek repentance for our past faults while upon the prayer cushion. It was upon prayer cushions that most of the great sages of the past attained enlightenment.

Photograph courtesy of Fo Guang Shan Monastery

I am a cushion. I have always been quite popular in China. We cushions have never been limited to only Buddhist monasteries and temples; we are found in many places. Every family—rich or poor, prominent or humble, large or small—makes use of us cushions.

I am called *putuan* in Chinese. *Pu* means "water grass" and *tuan* means "round." Originally, we cushions were made from rushes and were circular in shape, so that is how I got my name! We are used to keep clothing from getting dirty when kneeling and bowing. As the use of cushions spread to all parts of China, different kinds of materials were used in making us, and we were fashioned in many shapes and sizes. In temples today, you find cushions made from cotton and other material and in rectangular shapes on both long and short benches. But whatever the size, shape, and material, we are all called cushions!

Depending on their experience with Buddhist traditions, people will have different styles of bowing and showing devotion to the Buddhas. Beginners will often bob up and down quickly over and over, while the more experienced cultivators will usually take their time bowing reverently, humbly touching their foreheads to the cushion and gracefully uncurling the fingers of both hands with their palms facing up, open to the Buddha. I have found that people's level of cultivation is reflected in their manner of bowing. Experienced practitioners are quiet and composed when they pray, while beginners are more impatient and less focused.

Some beginners, not yet familiar with Buddhist etiquette, will enter the Great Hall through the middle door and kneel down on the cushion in the center of the hall. Both the middle door and cushion are reserved for use by the abbot and the monastic who presides over the Dharma service. It is as if beginners think that the Buddhas and bodhisattvas might not notice them if they kneel on the cushions that are placed to the side in the hall.

As a cushion, I am like a bridge between sentient beings and the Buddha Land, because I am in direct contact with the cultivators who come to the temple. I have first-hand knowledge of the benefits of Buddhist practice —especially of chanting and bowing. The sutras say, "Chanting the Buddha's name can eliminate unwholesome acts as numerous as grains of sand in a river. Bowing to the Buddha can bring boundless blessings and happiness." Cultivators usually sit on me to meditate with their eyes closed, chanting the Buddha's name. They also bow to the Buddha and kneel down on me to show their respect. I am very close to practitioners, because they use me so much.

Besides earning merit and bringing good fortune, bowing can improve a person's health and eliminate pride and other bad habits. Bowing is even said to be helpful for healing stomach ailments. I watch how the positive changes in the practitioners become encouragement for others. This allows people to be more receptive to the teachings of the Buddha. A final benefit is that, as people become more focused and aware, they have fewer intrusive thoughts, staying more in the present moment. I do not want to speak too much about the benefits of paying respect to the Buddhas and bodhisattvas. It is much better for people to put the teachings into practice in their own lives and experience the benefits for themselves.

It has troubled me to discover over the years that there are some disingenuous people in this world. These are the ones who kowtow to the Buddhas out of a less than candid piety. Instead, they make their prostrations in order to impress. This falsehood is demeaning to them, and it reflects poorly on the efforts of sincere cultivators. On one occasion, I heard an elder monastic telling a younger one that sincerity was not important when bowing to the Buddha. He said that what mattered most was to impress others! Fortunately, the young monastic realized the folly of this advice and vowed to do his bowing in private in order to avoid being criticized for impressing others in public.

Some practitioners who come to the temple go directly to pay their respects to the abbot and other senior monastics first. A few even come to visit with and pay their respects to their friends without even bothering to go and bow before the Buddha. If you think that it doesn't matter whether or not you venerate the Buddha before anyone else, then you are wrong. Your priority should be to put the Buddha in your mind before anyone else. The people who want to impress others and receive flattery place themselves and others above the Buddha. If this is your priority, then there is no need to learn loving-kindness and compassion from the Buddha—just allow yourself to be pulled down by the vanity of other people.

I hear people bragging about the number of times they chant a Buddha's name or how many times they bow each day. I am saddened by this, for this comes from a shallow wish to gain recognition and approval and not from a sincere devotion to the Buddha.

I have heard some say of Buddhism that its practitioners worship idols. I was shocked and worried when I first heard this, because if people were to stop honoring the Buddha, then what would happen to me. When I thought about the matter, though, I realized that such criticism is unnecessary, and generally comes from a lack of understanding. There is nothing unique about the intention behind this Buddhist practice. It is the same as with other religions and aspects of society from the highest institutions right on down to families in private homes. Christians have pictures of Jesus in their churches and homes, government offices have pictures of elected officials hanging on their walls, and many Chinese families have an ancestral tablet. Are these pictures and memorials all not displayed in honor of respected political and religious leaders and deceased family members? It is the same with Buddhism! We have statues of Buddhas and bodhisattvas to show honor and respect for the supreme teachers and shining exemplars who show us the Dharma path to enlightenment and whose lives embody the virtues of compassion and righteousness.

There are some people who are not Buddhist, but who still come to the temple to pay their respects to the Buddha. They do not understand the true meaning of bowing and making offerings. Instead, they prostrate and make offerings before the Buddha and bodhisattvas to petition for favors. What they ask for ranges from requests for more sons and grandsons to relief in times of hardship. I hope that the more experienced cultivators can help them to become aware of the true purpose of bowing and making offerings. Then those who are not Buddhists will be less likely to get the wrong idea about the Buddhist practice of bowing.

Bowing is only one method of cultivation. At one time, some monastics went out of the temple to cultivate. They attended funeral services to pray for the dead and in return, they received payment for this service. Understandably, some people were critical of this practice. Once there was a Chan master named Hanshan

Deqing, who used to officiate at funeral services. Walking home late one night, returning from a funeral service, an elderly couple was frightened by his sight. The wife was surprised that someone would be out walking in the middle of the night. Her husband told her that the only people out walking at that time of night were thieves or those attending funeral services. When Master Hanshan Deqing overheard this, he was offended to be placed in the same category as thieves. Upon reflection, however, he made a vow stating that he "would choose to die while seated upon a cushion in meditation rather than officiate at another funeral service." He went on to become a famous and much admired master.

Monastics take a vow to work to liberate all sentient beings and to toil for the ennoblement of humans. If they are unable to undertake the Mahayana path of Buddhism to liberate all sentient beings, at least "choosing to die while seated upon a cushion in meditation" will not bring harm upon Buddhism!

Candleholder

*Candles are one of the
ten offerings made to show
respect to the Buddha.
Without the traditional
offering of light,
we candleholders would not
be in such high demand.*

The candleholder, together with the incense burner and flower vase, are the typical offering vessels placed in front of the Buddha. Candleholders come in a rich profusion of shapes and styles and are typically decorated with auspicious symbols. Besides their function of providing light, lighting candles also symbolizes that the Buddha's light shines everywhere.

In ancient India oil lamps were commonly offered to the Buddha. When wax candles were developed, the unique "candleholder" vessel developed from a redesign of the oil lamp. Metal candleholders may be made from copper, iron, or tin, though there are also candleholders made from wood and stone. The wealthy sometimes had candleholders cast in gold and silver.

The main function of the candleholder is to keep the candle upright and easy to light. Candleholders increase the height of a candle and the distance it can illuminate, and they catch the dripping wax from the candle for safety and cleanliness.

C andles come in a variety of shapes and sizes, and so do candleholders. If you've visited a temple, made offerings to the Buddha, or have a family shrine at home, then you're certainly familiar with me. We candleholders are made from so many kinds of metals; we're even carved from wood. Candles are one of the ten offerings made to show respect to the Buddha. Without the traditional offering of light, we candleholders would not be in such high demand. You can see that candles and I are just like bosom buddies—inseparable you might say. There are as many different names for candles as there are shapes and sizes. The worshippers at the shrines of the city god and sea goddess only see normal size candles. But the devotees who go to Buddhist temples really get to see something special. They see huge one-thousand-pound candles with my friends and I standing as tall as a man!

With the advance of science, the candle is gradually being replaced by the electric light. Some modern monasteries located in large cities use lamps that are made to look like candles in candleholders. These lamps are very impressive, but when I first started seeing them, I couldn't understand why people didn't just use regular lights instead of lamps designed to look like candles. Were they trying to trick worshippers and the Buddha into thinking that they were offering candles? Eventually I came to understand that the point was to offer light, which, along with candles, could include any lamp or electric light. I decided that I could accept these changes as long as there was still a place for me! But what I couldn't accept was that some candles used in the temple were made from animal fat! Not only were people not accumulating merits using these candles, unwholesome karma was being created by the actual killing of the animals. The Buddha looks with compassion upon all sentient beings and must lament how foolish they are!

Not only am I used for holding candles but I'm also made for ornamental purposes. I'm placed at each side of the statue of the Buddha in the middle of the Great Hall. Sometimes things are busy in the monastery, and sometimes things are slow. The first and the fifteenth of each month and during special Dharma functions are my busiest times. During these events, people come from far and near to make offerings of incense and candles. When it's really busy, the monastic in charge of the offerings might rearrange or even remove some of the incense and candles that have been burning for a while to make room for the offerings of others.

One time, an elderly gentleman brought his son with him to the temple to pay their respects to the Buddha. Since there were many people making offerings that day, the monastic in charge removed the elderly man's candles not long after he had offered them. The man became upset thinking that he had wasted his money, so he took his son and left the temple. On their way home, the son was suddenly struck with an illness and died, leaving the father stricken by grief. The father bought a coffin and arranged to have his son's body sent home. When he reached his house, the father couldn't believe his eyes! Was that his son he saw waiting for him, or was it a ghost, he wondered. The son greeted him explaining how he had gotten lost in the midst of the many pilgrims at the temple and returned home by himself. The old man looked at the coffin. He cautiously opened it. Inside, instead of his son's body, the old man found two large candles just like the ones he had offered at the temple. Placed on top of the candles was a small piece of paper with characters written on it. "These were not offered with sincerity," the old man read. "Return to the owner." At that moment, the man realized the message of the returned candles. He realized that when making offerings what matters most to the Buddhas and the bodhisattvas is an honest and sincere heart. It's not important how long the offerings sit on the altar.

There have been times in the past when people haven't needed me. At one time people carried my candle friends in lanterns, allowing the travelers of old to make their way in the darkness. Today people have the convenience of flashlights, but now few want to get out and enjoy the beauty and mystery of nature. Many would rather spend their evenings in nightclubs, indulging in sensual pleasures. In ancient times candles not only brought light to darkness but were also believed to protect from evil. When candles burn, they drip wax that looks just like falling teardrops. Sadly, the light from candles is not strong enough to illuminate the whole world. I have seen misguided people spreading the seeds of unwholesomeness and ignorance—lying, stealing, and seeking sensual pleasure. When I see this happening, how can I contain my tears? What greater sacrifice can a candle make than to burn itself out serving humanity and bringing light to the darkness of the Saha world?

While candles are symbols of light and purity, the Saha world still contains evil and darkness. An egregious example of this evil is something that was practiced long ago. Criminals would be covered with oil, set on fire, and burned like candles. They would suffer horrible deaths! I care deeply about the dignity of all sentient beings. The anguish I felt at this treatment of people at the hands of their fellow human beings just melted my heart with sorrow.

In ending my story, I want to remind everyone that when making an offering to the Buddha, a sincere and honest heart is what is important, no matter what form of light is used—an electric lamp light or the light from a candle. Finally, I exhort everyone to be mindful of the sacrifice of the candle. Work to spread the light of the Buddha's teachings and to illuminate the darkness of the Saha world!

Commemorative
Tablet

I must warn you against saying,
"I am young" or "I am healthy."
No one knows what
tomorrow will bring!
I have witnessed the death
of many a young and healthy person.
I urge you to practice and work diligently.

A commemorative tablet is a rectangular tablet made of wood upon which is inscribed the name of the person being remembered during offering ceremonies. First developed during the Eastern Han dynasty (25-220 CE), this custom originated in Confucian ritual in which the official title and name of the deceased would be inscribed upon a rectangular tablet of wood about ten to forty centimeters long, serving as a place where the spirit of the deceased could find repose. The custom was later adopted by Buddhists as well.

In Buddhist temples and monasteries, the commemorative tablets in the Longevity Hall are called auspicious tablets for long life, while those in the Hall of Virtue are called tablets for the deceased. Tablets made for living persons are generally made from red paper, while tablets made for the deceased are chiefly made from yellow paper. So one could even say that the red paper and the yellow paper delineate the boundary between life and death.

In households throughout my homeland, tablets have been arrayed on family altars generation after generation. Monasteries and temples have also upheld the tradition of placing both longevity tablets and memorial tablets for ancestors in special rooms that are dedicated to the different types of tablets. Tablets written on behalf of the living are kept in the Longevity Hall. The memorial tablets written in honor of the dead are preserved in the Hall of Virtue. I have the distinction of being the tablet. The name characters for family members and friends—both the living and the dead—are written upon us. This is the way families remember and venerate their ancestors. Also through me, the memories of the wise teachers of the past remain alive in the hearts and minds of people. We tablets are constructed from either paper or wood, but it makes no difference whether I am paper or wood. What is truly important is the depth of a person's sincerity and the level of their respect. I am used to recall the kind deeds of elderly family members and to venerate those who pass away. If there is also a renowned teacher or someone whom you admire whose actions and beliefs you respect and seek to emulate, you can show your esteem with me—the tablet.

Sometimes, the heir to a family fortune turns out to be a lazy spendthrift. When this happens, he starts squandering his inheritance, but I am here right in front of his eyes. As he looks at me—the memorial tablet to his ancestors—he can think about all the hard work and sacrifice that went into establishing the family business and making it prosper. Then the wastrel should be overcome with shame and regret. At this point, hopefully, he will change his ways and become a hardworking productive member of his family and society.

As a child, Wen Tianxiang[5] would play at a nearby temple, where he saw the tablets honoring the patriarchs, sages, and saints that were accorded a place of honor and respect on the altar. He made a vow that one day his tablet would stand shoulder-to-shoulder with them. As a man, he was loyal to his country and did much good for it and its people. I think everyone would agree with me that, as a memorial tablet, I can be very educational!

In addition to the tablets for longevity and the memorial tablets for ancestors, there have been other types of us. In the days of dynastic rule, every family had an "emperor's tablet," on which was written "Long live the emperor!" Today I live in a republic, and I carry the words, "Long live the nation!" The desire for the longevity of a single emperor has progressed to the wish for the well being of all people in the entire nation. I feel that all people are standing in solidarity with me. Gladness is inscribed on every line of my heart.

Another type of tablet, the "appreciation tablet," is one whose job is to memorialize a family's benefactor. The name characters of the benefactor are written on me and offerings of incense and pure water are made every day. Because of me, family members are able to faithfully keep in mind the benefactor's contribution to the family. But, oh, how times can change! Nowadays, people have found a new use for us tablets. The names and birthdates of people's enemies are written on us and curses are uttered daily in hopes that their enemies will meet with an untimely death. To wish life for those we love and death for those we hate is a result of the ongoing mundane struggle of our discriminating mind.

Photograph by Ven. Hui Rong

Wise Confucius has his own memorial tablet. It is called the "Tablet of the Supreme Saintly Teacher." There is also a tablet of the widely revered founder and father of the Republic of China, President Sun Yat-sen. It is called the "Portrait of the Father of Our Nation." The tablet has a picture of him on it. When people see the tablet dedicated to Confucius, they ponder the principles for maintaining a moral society, and the picture of President Sun Yat-sen on his memorial tablet provides a constant reminder to everyone of the hardship and great sacrifice it takes to have freedom.

Now I have to give advice to people who refuse to show respect to heroes because they say this amounts to idolatry. The fact is that everybody performs some form of "idol worship." For example, when you bring to mind feelings of respect for your parents, your parents are your idols. When you believe in Jesus, Jesus is your idol. When you pray to God with the wish that He will take you to heaven, then God and Heaven are your idols. Unless you can claim that you are not a part of the human race, then you, too, perform some type of "idol" worship. No one can truthfully make the claim that they do not venerate idols.

While we tablets are most often employed as a means of displaying honor and respect, sometimes people do press us into service in their attempts to ward off natural disasters, bad luck, and death. In some areas of the land where we tablets are used, superstitious people hold ceremonies to invite the spirits of the deceased, for fear that we tablets may lack spirits. But we are also used to express compassion for a lonely ghost, or even, simply, universal compassion for all beings. I must make the point, though, that there is a big difference between enlisting us tablets as an aid for showing respect and misusing us as a medium for causing fear!

My services are not requested much nowadays at funerals. With the advent of photography, the need for tablets has almost been written off. Today during funeral and memorial services, a photo of the departed loved one often replaces the tablet. Using a picture instead of a tablet enables the mourners to feel closer to the departed family member. Memorial tablets are made of yellow paper and longevity tablets use red paper. The Hall of Virtue, the usual place for memorial tablets, and the Longevity Hall, the usual place for longevity tablets, are located on opposite sides of the Great Hall. This symbolizes that life and death are not very far from each another.

Cremation has also become popular. During this service, the use of the tablet is often eliminated because the ashes and bone fragments are placed in an urn upon which the person's name and date of birth and death are written. The most common place for keeping urns is in a columbarium located near a temple. Sometimes you will see a few tablets in front of an urn. Mourners will weep at the sight because the dead are separated from family, friends, and loved ones.

I must warn you against saying, "I am young" or "I am healthy." No one knows what tomorrow will bring! I have witnessed the death of many a young and healthy person. I urge you to practice and work diligently. Do not squander your time. There is an adage that cautions: "Do not wait until old age to do your spiritual cultivation; the graveyards are full of young people." After all, what I really hope deep in my heart is not to have the names of the living or the deceased inscribed upon me, but the words "Revival of the True Buddhist Spirit." That would give me a joyous heart.

Photograph by Ven. Hui Rong

Ordination Certificate

Aspirants were required to take precepts,
that is, they had to vow to follow
certain practices in their lives.
Only after taking the precepts,
would they receive their
Certificates of Ordination.
Those unable to take the precepts
were not qualified to become monastics.

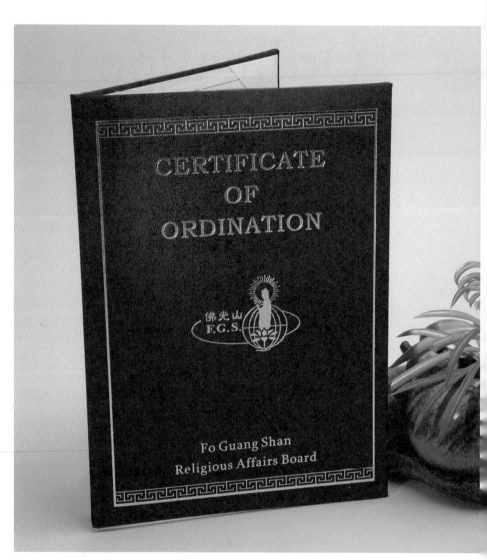

Photograph by Chih-Cheng Chang

The ordination certificate is a document issued after a male or female monastic has received full ordination, and functions as an identification card and travel passport for monastics. Its origins are in Tang dynasty China, when in the year 856 CE Emperor Xuanzong decreed that the Venerable Bianzhang, a Buddhist monk be the head of the religions of Buddhism, Daoism, and Confucianism. Venerable Bianzhang created a system in which monks and nuns would be given certificates upon ordination.

During the Tang and Song dynasties, monastics had to obtain an "ordination license" as soon as they entered the monastic order, and then received an ordination certificate upon later obtaining full ordination. Both the license and the certificate were issued by the government, and one's ordination license was inspected before full ordination, and an ordination certificate.

During the Qing dynasty Emperor Yongzheng (r. 1722-1735 CE) abolished the ordination license, allowing people to seek ordination without restriction. Ordination certificates were then given by monasteries themselves rather than the government, and began to be issued in much greater numbers. The practice of monasteries granting ordination certificates continues to today.

One day while still a child, Master Xuanzang⁶ went to visit his brother, who had left home to become a monk at a Pure Land temple. Xuanzang felt drawn to the peace and purity of the hallowed main shrine and was filled with awe and respect for the monastics. Right then and there, a seed was planted in his heart. Later he vowed to become a monk himself so that he could cultivate Buddhism, propagate the Dharma, and benefit sentient beings.

When he became a young man, Xuanzang went to Luoyang to take the examination to become a monk. He was very disappointed to learn that he was not qualified to receive the certification because he was not yet twenty years old. At that time, the Certification by Examination was equivalent to our present day Certification of Ordination. Feeling unsettled by this experience and not wishing to leave, he lingered at the temple. Zhen, an official in the city noticed the despondent young aspirant. "Why are you still here?" inquired the official.

Xuanzang spoke up without hesitation. "I want to receive my certification and become a monk."

"Why do you want to be a monk?" Zhen probed, truly interested.

"I wish to dedicate my life's work to following the Tathagata, to study and spread his teachings," replied Xuanzang.

The official was so moved by Xuanzang's sincere determination that he made an exception and conferred certification right on the spot. After becoming a monk, Xuanzang spent many years in India, traveling and collecting sutras. He eventually returned to

China with the sutras, where he spent the rest of his life translating them, enriching Chinese Buddhism and culture in the process. Xuanzang was a monk during the end of the Sui dynasty and the beginning of the Tang dynasty. The change from Certificate by Examination to Certificate of Ordination is believed to have occurred at this time, during the reign of the Tang emperor, Xuanzong.[7] This change strengthened the ordination system. Aspirants were required to take precepts, that is, they had to vow to follow certain practices in their lives. Only after taking the precepts, would they receive their Certificates of Ordination. Those unable to take the precepts were not qualified to become monastics.

This process of ordination was strictly adhered to until the beginning of the Qing dynasty. Gradually, for a variety of reasons, the rule regarding receiving ordination only after having taken the precepts was relaxed. During this period, poor people who had great difficulty scratching out a living, started becoming monastics as a means of survival. Criminals were even known to buy ordination certificates and hide out in temples.

Later, during another time of political and economic upheaval, the government implemented the practice of selling ordination certificates as a means of generating revenue. Sadly, the government treated me as a commodity rather than as a means of insuring that those ordained as monastics had the proper qualifications. This corruption of the ordination system resulted in severe inconsistencies in the personal character of monastics, their commitment to spreading the Dharma, and the depth of their cultivation. In the mid-twentieth century, Chinese Buddhism was in a grave situation, due, in part, to this ruinous system of issuing ordination certificates by some Buddhist officials, as well as the political decisions of the government.

Photographs courtesy of Fo Guang Shan Monastery

Oh, pardon me! Allow me to introduce myself and tell you what I look like. I am made of special paper, the same kind that is used for university diplomas. However, my paper is even more beautiful and quite expensive. When lay people earn their diplomas, they are able to get a better job or make more money. However when monastics receive their certificates, they are able to seek enlightenment and became ordained members of the sangha. But just as some students study to gain knowledge, while others simply desire the diploma, some monastics seek enlightenment, while others strive only to take the precepts and get their certificates of ordination.

If asked about my importance, I would not hesitate to say that I am just as important to a monastic as an identification card is to the ordinary citizen. Without your I. D. card, when traveling you cannot spend the night at a hotel, and without their ordination certificate monastics cannot stay at other temples and monasteries. Some people say that I am just a meal ticket, because when monastics travel to different monasteries, it does not matter if they have as many as twelve precept scars on their heads, the monk in charge of the guests always wants to see the certificate of ordination. Without me the visiting monks will be turned away.

Prior to taking the precepts and receiving the ordination certificate, a monastic is required to participate in a precepts retreat. The monastics remember this special experience all of their lives. The retreat is taken very seriously, and much is expected of the participants. Usually the retreat lasts one to two months. In my opinion, this is not very long, but whatever the length of time, the participants must be diligent, attentive, and focused. The Buddhist monastic system requires that monastics practice and follow the precepts for five years, and then they are permitted to learn the teachings and practice Chan meditation.

In the past, large monasteries had special halls just for studying the precepts. We cannot compare that time to the present. Today many monasteries do not stress the importance of studying the precepts. Often only a few days are spent in the precepts retreat. The new monastic is happy to receive me, but before taking the precepts, I have to wonder, does he deeply understand the meaning of the precepts? After taking the precepts, does he really comprehend the value of the precepts? Under these conditions, has this monastic truly received the precepts?

I want to tell everyone that when you take the precepts, you are not merely receiving a certificate. You are receiving the spirit and the essence of the precepts. You should follow the instruction of each precept and make that spirit, that essence, a part of your daily life. If you do not do that, then your life as a monastic is not only an insult to me but also causes injury to the character and reputation of the sangha.

The precepts are not only the spirit and heart of monastic life, they are the guidelines for right conduct. Without precepts, monastics will not develop the proper character. Today, there are many monastics who have not taken the precepts, do not have certificates of ordination, and, consequently, do not know or understand the proper conduct and correct behavior required. These "monastics" are actively involved in monasteries and proclaim themselves to be "Dharma teachers."

I have to mention that during the Certificate of Ordination ceremony the age of the monastic is not emphasized. After receiving the certificate, the only age that is emphasized is the number of years a monastic has been ordained. My hope is that people will honor the precepts. Before he entered final nirvana, the Buddha told us to "follow the precepts as your teacher." Let us all remember the Buddha's last words.

I sincerely pray that after the monastics receive me, they will be models for the lay community. They must be the pillars of Buddhism. Finally, I hope that people are allowed to take the precepts only when they are qualified and prepared and that the days of randomly issuing certificates of ordination are over.

Fo Guang Shan Temple
CERTIFICATE OF ORDINATION

Date of Issue: December 24, 2008   Ref.No: M004

This is to certify that _____,

(Full Name: _____)

from _____, born on _____,

became a monastic under ___Venerable Master Hsing Yun___ of

___Fo Guang Shan Temple___, and was ordained at Fo Guang Shan Hsi Lai Temple in America. He has successfully completed the requisite training and participated in the Sramanera Ordination Ceremony on December 14, the Upasampada Ordination Ceremony on December 20, and the Bodhisattva Ordination Ceremony on December 24 of the Year 2008, and has solemnly vowed to uphold the precepts for life. The Ten Most Venerable Masters hereby duly certify and confer this Ordination Certificate to the above-named participant. We sincerely hope that the Triple Gem will witness this and the heavenly nagas will render endless protection to him.

Sila Upadhyaya: Most Venerable Master Hsing Yun

Karma Acarya: Most Venerable Hsin Ting

Instructing Acarya: Most Venerable Long Xiang

Witnessing Acaryas: Venerable Hui Long   Venerable Long Yin

Venerable Hui Chuan   Venerable Hui Kuan

Venerable Hui Dao   Venerable Di Ru

Venerable Hui Yi

Ceremony Acarya: Venerable Hsin Pei

Deputy Ceremony Acarya: Venerable Hui Chi   Venerable Hui Chao

佛光山

茲有   字

生於西元   年

依　佛光山　寺上

美國西來寺，於西元二〇

戒，十二月二十日晉比丘

戒，經三師七證白四羯磨

犯，並經壇上十師審核合

實證明，龍天永護。

得戒阿闍黎   上星下雲 大和尚

羯磨阿闍黎   上心下定 和　尚

教授阿闍黎   上隆下相 和　尚

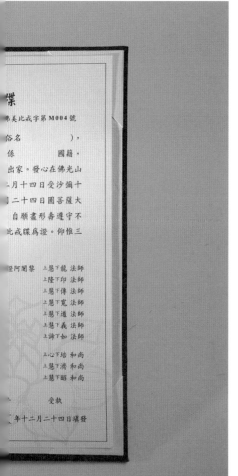

牒

佛美比戒字第 M004 號

俗名   ）,

係   國籍,

出家。發心在佛光山

二月十四日受沙彌十

二十四日圓菩薩大

自願盡形壽遵守不

比戒牒為證。仰惟三

登阿闍黎　上慧下龍 法師
　　　　　上陸下印 法師
　　　　　上慧下傳 法師
　　　　　上慧下寬 法師
　　　　　上慧下道 法師
　　　　　上慧下義 法師
　　　　　上諦下如 法師

　　　　　上心下培 和尚
　　　　　上慧下濟 和尚
　　　　　上慧下昭 和尚

　　受執

年十二月二十四日填發

Photograph by
Chih-Cheng Chang

Wenshu Report

*Many people use us
wenshu reports
as if we are passports to the
Western Pure Land!
When a person dies,
the family will recite sutras, pray,
and then burn me, believing that
the deceased can use me to get
into the Western Pure Land.*

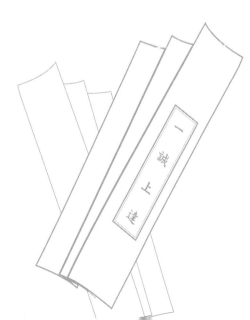

A wenshu report is a document which records the merits of the devotees attending a Dharma service. The wenshu report is used to make a declaration to all the Buddhas and bodhisattvas, and is usually read out loud by the presiding monastic or the discipline master.

There are two main types of wenshu reports. Those written on red paper are called "wenshu reports for longevity," while those written on white or yellow paper are called "wenshu reports for the deceased." Wenshu reports for longevity are further divided into those composed for disaster relief, auspicious blessings, or prayers for peace. Wenshu reports for the deceased are intended to seek liberation for the dead and pray for blessings upon them.

Many people have seen me, but they might not have known that my name is Wenshu. Some people called me a "report" or a "transfer of merits document." The terms "report" and "transfer of merits document" are popular in Taiwan and *wenshu* report is popular in China. Perhaps being called by two names is why, for as long as I can recall, I've had an identity problem—always feeling torn between how my past is viewed and my own vision of myself. I know I'm destined for great things, if only...well, let me tell you my story.

It all started during the days of the imperial dynasties, when an official wanted to communicate with the emperor. At that time the official had to prepare a written report containing his comments, suggestions, or proposals. These reports would be taken to the emperor in hopes of gaining an audience. This method of corresponding with the emperor became the model for communicating with the Buddha and bodhisattvas.

People listed their accumulated merits on me, which were then presented to the Buddha and bodhisattvas. I was supposed to be what today would be called a "red phone" between people and the Buddha. But the calls that people made through me were never answered. The Dharma body of all Buddhas permeates all space and time! The Buddha isn't some kind of bookkeeper—simply keeping track of people's merits! The conditions of our lives are determined by our karma, in this and previous lives. People can't escape the law of cause and effect, though many have thought otherwise and asked me to report to the Buddha for them. Every time I was sent to make a report, I had to wonder what the compassionate Buddha thought about this practice.

There are several kinds of us *wenshu* reports. We *wenshu* reports written on red paper are called "*wenshu* reports for longevity," and we *wenshu* reports written on yellow or white paper are called "*wenshu* reports for the deceased." We red ones are used to prevent disasters and to petition for good fortune and safety. We yellow and white ones are used to help ensure a good rebirth.

Many people use us *wenshu* reports as if we are passports to the Western Pure Land! When a person dies, the family will recite sutras, pray, and then burn me, believing that the deceased can use me to get into the Western Pure Land. People misguidedly believe that I'm a ticket to the Pure Land of Ultimate Bliss. I must say, though, that I have adored the monastics who have placed me in a position of honor. They are like governmental officials in charge of issuing passports and visas. However, I did have my doubts about them being actual ambassadors for Amitabha Buddha. If the deceased haven't accumulated good karma, there is no getting into the Pure Land!

Wenshu reports for longevity are used to offer prayers for the living. The presiding monastic will kneel down in front of the Buddha and read the prayers written on the *wenshu*. I know that monastics are caring and compassionate toward people, but some of them show little concern for their role as monastics or for the decline of Buddhism. Sometimes they don't seem to care if, because of their actions, Buddhism suffers. They just lower themselves to the level of a drummer in a funeral procession. When I see this, it looks as if they are selling life insurance for the living or running funeral homes for the dead! I can only weep with sadness for the Buddha and these deluded followers.

Just as governmental documents had to be stamped with an official seal to be valid, we *wenshu* reports went through the same process. The stamp imprinted on us used the characters "Triple Gem"—the Buddha, the Dharma and the Sangha. I seriously question whether the monastics who only performed funeral services, without preaching the Dharma, could claim to be true members of the sangha.

It didn't make sense to me that they would stamp me with "Triple Gem." Show me the sutra where the Buddha says that, for the Dharma to be valid, you need to be stamped with an official seal! When the Buddha was alive, he communicated with people. He didn't need an official stamp to validate the truth of his teachings. However, during this period, his followers, acting in his name, used stamps and were not even ashamed of what they were doing. I feel great sorrow for the Buddha because of what I saw his followers doing. Even if the Buddha had used an official stamp, he couldn't help but cry seeing the abuses propagated in his name by his followers today—issuing entry permits into the Pure Land for the dead and life insurance policies for the living!

Some monastics and lay people alike, who knew the Buddha's teachings well and faithfully followed the Dharma, did not like what I was used for and looked down on me. They felt that my use was not in keeping with the true spirit of Buddhism. But I was innocent! The so-called devotees who had turned Buddhism into a business exploited me as their lackey. How could I have changed their actions when their minds were clouded by greed and ignorance?

I wanted to be of service in spreading the Dharma and Buddhist culture. I had hoped my paper would be used for printing sutras or Buddhist magazines. But that was not my fate. There were plenty of temples in the funeral business, and they continued to stock large amounts of us *wenshu* for their funeral services or other rituals. We *wenshu* reports continued to be printed. If we weren't used for funerals then we were used for other purposes. There were devotees that admired us and believed in the efficacy of our use. They thought that when they accumulated merits through participation in funeral services or other rituals they had to use me to list all their merits. Without me, they believed, the Buddha wouldn't know of their merits and wouldn't keep a record of them. Consequently, even though knowledgeable cultivators didn't approve of me, I had my own followers in secular life and was still popular.

In Taiwan, I have been very popular during the spring and autumnal memorial Dharma functions. Some non-traditional Buddhist temples were influenced by Daoism. These temples would list donors' names on *wenshu* reports, giving the donors various titles based on how much money was donated.

From the perspective of the Dharma, we can laugh at how superstitious people can be. Sometimes the monastic at the services had to read to the Buddha from the *wenshu* report several times a day—up to three times for someone who had died. I thought that if the Buddha and bodhisattvas really were in charge of these matters, they would be kept very busy, indeed, and probably be a little upset at having to listen to all those repetitions. If a dead person had gone to hell because of his criminal actions, the outcome wouldn't change, regardless of how many repetitions were made. I wondered whether the King of Hell would let the deceased have a drop of sweet dew to ease his thirst. There are not many people in the monastery capable of practicing the law of cause and effect, but quite a few are very good at writing *wenshu* reports for the deceased. It has never been my desire to occupy this position, and I hope the monastics will change this tradition.

Buddhist Beads

They would count one bead
for each recitation.
When a practitioner would
complete the daily chanting,
there would be a sense of
accomplishment, and
I would receive a grateful smile.

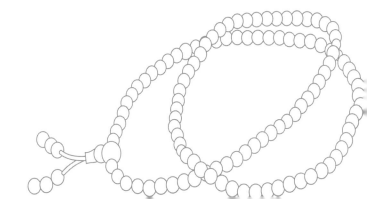

Also called recitation beads, chanting beads, counting beads, or mantra beads, Buddhist beads are carried by practitioners while reciting the name of Amitabha Buddha or chanting mantras. They also represent merit, Buddha nature, compassion, goodness, auspiciousness, perfection, and the Buddha mind. Besides acting as a reminder to not do unwholesome things, they are also a proper form of adornment.

Buddhist beads can be made to be worn as a bracelet, carried in the hand, or worn as a necklace. The sutras recommend various numbers of beads per string, including 108, 54, 42, and 21 beads. The beads themselves are made of such materials as bodhi seeds, crystal, sandalwood, carnelian, amber, gold, silver, and pearl.

When reciting, the beads are held in the hand, and starting with the bead next to the mother bead (the largest bead of the set), the practitioner carefully slides one bead aside with a pinching motion for each recitation of Amitabha Buddha's name, a Buddhist scripture, or mantra. Divider beads, if they are present, are not counted, and when the mother bead is reached once again one rarely goes past it, but instead reverses direction. In wearing Buddhist beads, practitioners are mainly reminding themselves to always keep up the practice of reciting Amitabha Buddha's name diligently, and further practice Buddhism in daily life.

There is not a person who is untouched by the eight sufferings of this Saha world. Even if you live in a mansion and feast on delicacies, you cannot escape the suffering that comes from birth, sickness, old age, and death. That is why many wise practitioners use me for chanting. I help them to single-mindedly focus attention on their recitation. Through this practice, when cultivators die, they are able to go to the Western Pure Land of Ultimate Bliss.

The way we Buddhist beads are made is quite unusual. Some people go to the seashore to pick up coral to make us. Many jewelry stores sell Buddha beads made from precious materials, such as pearls, agate, amber and crystal. Some people use naturally-grown *bodhi* seeds. These are round like the moon and the surface of the seeds seems to contain countless tiny stars.

Using Buddha beads has many benefits. Originally, practitioners used me to count the number of times they recited the Buddha's name. Many devotees would chant the Buddha's name up to twenty thousand times a day. Through chanting the Buddha's name, they felt calm, peaceful, and in control of their wandering mind. They would count one bead for each recitation. When a practitioner would complete the daily chanting, there would be a sense of accomplishment, and I would receive a grateful smile. If the daily practice was missed because of laziness or forgetfulness, when the practitioner saw me, I would be a reminder of their negligence!

I feel sad when I see how many people misuse me. Due to ignorance, they think that, by displaying prayer beads draped around their necks or holding them in their hands, they will be seen as very pious. These people cast me aside most of the time, but when visitors come to call, they bring me out and start chanting. Not even chanting is free from the sanctimoniousness of the Saha world.

Long ago, the lower ranking monastics were not even allowed to openly hold me in their hands or wear me around their necks. I wondered about this. Why couldn't all monastics freely use Buddha beads when chanting? Now, thank goodness, everyone is equal in the Dharma.

Some lay people like to wear prayer beads around their necks and on their wrists to show that they are Buddhists. Consequently, many buy beads as gifts to give to other Buddhists. It's a lot like the way people give moon cakes as gifts during the Moon Festival.[8] I am truly honored to be given as a gift.

People do have different opinions about me, though. Some consider me old fashioned because I am so often used by elderly people. This view reflects a lack of understanding. Often young people don't pay much attention to me until they start to grow old. That's when they really get interested in me.

Traditionally the abbot of the monastery wears a beautiful string of Buddha beads around his neck. Sometimes the monastics who only perform funeral services will also buy beautiful beads, but they don't actually use me as an aid for chanting. Instead, they use me as jewelry or decoration, trying to make themselves look superior. It's not good for Buddhism when I'm misused.

People tend to assume that those holding Buddha beads are good people because of my long history. I have a reputation for keeping good company. Sometimes this is a big mistake. Appearances can be deceiving! I remember one occasion when a monastic and I were traveling on a train. One of the passengers had stolen a lot of money from another passenger. When the police came through the train to investigate, the thief had a clever idea. He quickly grabbed me from the monastic, closed his eyes, and started moving his lips. The police officer passed us by. He must have thought to himself, that fellow sitting and chanting next to the monk must be a Buddhist, too... he wouldn't steal from another person... he couldn't be the suspect... I'll leave him alone. It's very hard for people to see the falseness of those who misuse me. Thinking about what happened on the train really makes me worry deeply about my reputation. Misuses of me must stop!

I take great displeasure in one kind of person. He holds me in his hand when chanting the Buddha's name, which is fine with me, but what does bother me, is when he keeps moving me with his fingers and talking with other people at the same time. I really don't understand this. Does he wish me to count his sentences while he talks to other people? I implore you to protect my noble calling by not misusing me.

I remember one occasion that was quite humorous. A layperson, Mr. Liu, was coming to meet with the abbot. He had a string of prayer beads around his neck. As Mr. Liu approached the monastery gate, he suddenly held his hand out in front of his chest. He started walking around pompously as if he were an actor on the stage of a Chinese opera. People laughed at him. While the scene was quite comical, I was also embarrassed for him. How could he study Buddhism and act so strangely at the same time?

Sincerely, I wish to speak to all of you who are Buddhist cultivators. Chanting the name of the Buddha has to come from your heart. Whether or not you use me is unimportant. Cultivation has to be a part of your daily life. I'm sure you can see that using beads for decoration or jewelry, putting on pompous airs, and moving your lips pretending to recite the Buddha's name are not examples of true cultivation.

Sincere Buddhism practitioners! Please save me! Do not let me be just an ornament anymore. I only want to be a tool to help people purify their minds on the path to enlightenment.

Haiqing

*"Gracefully moving are the
wide dancing sleeves,
Like the ocean-blue birds
coming from the China Sea."*

*Disciples look so graceful and
solemn when they wear me
that long ago people started
calling me a haiqing.*

The haiqing, "ocean blue," is a traditional Chinese robe with wide sleeves. Its waist, lower hem, and sleeves are all loose and wide, making it very comfortable to wear, and it became the style of dress worn by both Buddhist monastics and laity when paying homage to the Buddha. There is a line by the famous Tang poet Li Bai that praises the beauty of the haiqing:

> *Gracefully moving are the wide dancing sleeves,*
> *Like the ocean-blue birds coming from the China Sea.*

The haiqing is also called a dapao, "big robe." It was adopted by ancient Chan temples because it's cloth is expansive like the ocean, able to encompass all phenomena, and the graceful waves of its billowing fabric represent unimpeded freedom. The color blue in the name is an allusion to the adage that "blue dye comes from indigo, but surpasses it in color," just as students surpass their masters generation after generation. It is encouragement to put forth greater effort.

Today the haiqing comes in two colors: black is worn by most Buddhist followers when paying homage to the Buddha, while yellow is worn by the abbot of the temple or the monastic officiating during a Dharma service.

Some call me Han clothing, some call me a *haiqing*, and still others call me the "big robe." I received the name of Han clothing because, in ancient China, the Han people wore clothes that looked very similar to me. In Buddhism, disciples wear me when bowing before the Buddha and reciting sutras. Disciples look so graceful and solemn when they wear me that long ago people started calling me a *haiqing*. The term "*haiqing*" comes from the name of a large, elegant, and graceful bird found along the shore of Liaodong, China. When this bird spreads its wings, it looks just like my sleeves, so people borrowed the name of this bird to refer to me. During the Tang dynasty, the famous poet Li Bai once praised me in his poetry: "Gracefully moving are the wide dancing sleeves, Like the ocean-blue birds coming from the China Sea." I am designed differently from other monastic clothing. I am cut large and wide and hang loosely at the waist, sleeves and lower part of my gown. This is why I am also called the "big robe."

In ancient China, the monastics as well as the laity wore me as their everyday attire. As China became influenced by the West, Chinese dress gradually became Westernized. Lay people no longer wore a *haiqing* every day. Nowadays, you will not see me anymore unless you go to a monastery or the Chinese opera. At one time, there was a famous photo that showed a man with a bald head wearing a robe that looked a lot like me. People thought he was a famous monk, but when you looked closely, it was clear that he was Wu Qingyuan, a famous *weiqi* master! He had been residing in Japan for many years. People realized that Japan had kept the tradition of wearing ancient Chinese clothing, while the Westernized Chinese had not!

Do not think that I am just a round-collared, square-cut robe. Wearing me could change your status, and people might not recognize you. I remember once when a layperson went to the temple for a Dharma function. His head was shaved like a monk, and as he walked into the temple wearing a *haiqing*, some pilgrims thought he was an actual monk and gave him red envelopes containing alms. Sigh! I had become a billboard for collecting money! On another occasion, seven monastics were officiating at Yogacara Flaming Mouth ceremonies.[10] When they saw that they were two monastics short, they had no choice but to find two lay persons who knew how to blow the horn and beat the drum. The recruits were given *haiqings* and dressed up as monastics so that they could help with the service. When people wear the *haiqing*, no one dares to question whether the person is or is not a monastic.

In some places, so-called monks wear Western-style suits without giving me a thought. I have seen some looking quite like dandies sporting fancy red and green ties and wearing fedora hats. No one would guess that they were monks. If a temple benefactor were to invite one of these Westernized monks to recite a sutra, the monk would have to become like Sun Wukong—the Monkey King[11] performing seventy-two transformations—putting on a *haiqing* and suddenly becoming a respectable monk!

It is well known that there are no sleeves as big as mine. There is a marvelous story regarding my big sleeves. During the reign of Emperor Wu of the Liang dynasty,[12] the emperor's wife, Chishi was not a Buddhist and always found fault with the monastics. She took pleasure in making false accusations against them. On one occasion, she invited Master Baozhi and his disciples to a banquet, and arranged to have pork stuffed into the buns that were going to be served. If the master and his followers had eaten the pork buns, they would have broken the precepts against eating meat and their reputations would have been tarnished. But if they did not eat the pork buns, they would be insulting the emperor's consort. During these despotic times, such actions could result in the master and his followers being beheaded.

But Master Baozhi's wisdom was very deep. He realized what was going on. Before the meal was served, he instructed his disciples to enlarge the sleeves of their *haiqings* and hide meatless steamed buns in their sleeves. During the banquet they exchanged the meatless buns for the pork buns! In this way they were able to evade the trap that the Empress Chishi had set for them. Although only a legend, this story shows that my big sleeves are far from being useless.

Just as soldiers are required to wear uniforms when on duty and when meeting superior officers, monastics are required to wear me when participating in Dharma functions and when meeting with the senior monastics. When a senior monastic comes to a Dharma function not wearing me, another might see this and say, "I am not wearing my *haiqing* either." It means: If a monastic is not wearing me, he is not showing proper respect for the sangha. I am the symbol of respect; monastics cannot do without me.

Originally, I was a formal and venerated robe. Monastics were supposed to wear me when prostrating before the Buddha, reciting sutras, and when meeting with others. Some of the more senior meditation practitioners even wore me when they went out shopping so that they would reflect the graceful walking of their meditation practice. The so-called new generation has already forgotten the history and tradition of wearing me though, and they laugh and make fun of the monastics wearing such strange, old-fashioned clothing to the marketplace. The younger monastics reacted to this ridicule by refusing to wear me under any circumstances. New monastic clothing, called *arhat* clothes,[13] was cleverly created and became popular for a while, so people were wearing me less. How could I not be anxious, seeing my power descending like a sunset! I wondered if I would gradually perish.

You might have heard about the movement in Buddhism to reform monastic clothing? Many people found reasons to oppose me. They felt that I used too much cloth, I was too expensive, too loose and big, not neat, inconvenient to wear when working, and that Han clothing was not an essential part of Chinese Buddhism. People wanted to get rid of me and design new monastic attire. A year before he died, Master Taixu[14] gave a few newly designed monastic robes to Master Yuanyan, who ordered the production

of new monastic attire according to Master Taixu's design. In this way, he hoped to show his support for reforming monastic attire. But some conservative monks argued that the current monastic attire was part of a priceless tradition, and they advocated that the traditional monastic attire not be abolished. The new and old were debating with each other! Since there was disagreement within the reform movement, and since China was on the verge of war, the question of reforming me was put on hold. Eventually, my life went on as before.

Originally, I was meant to be made from dyed cloth, and only in the colors of black or gray when worn by monastics. This was to avoid flashy colors. In some places, the monks and nuns wore clothes that clashed with the original intention. Those monks would wear *haiqings* during funeral services that were colored blue, red, yellow, green, or even multiple colors. They dressed as if they were actors performing on a stage, and as they came out onto their stage, many followers trailed behind them wearing dazzling, multicolored clothes and carrying flags and umbrellas. Some nuns even wore wooden clogs, their silk *haiqings* dyed white or black, dancing back and forth in the air like butterflies. Even the dress of fashionable young ladies is not as colorful!

The last thing I want to tell you is that I hope the monastics who want to reform monastic attire will reconsider my role. Let the clothing used for daily wear be modified, but do not change me. I should remain as formal attire. I should continue to be worn, but only for Dharma functions and formal occasions. Do not wear me as casual attire and do not make me colorful, as if competing with the clothing worn by fashionable young ladies of the opera. All I ask is to be kept economical and simple. Then I will dance with hands and feet of joy and a voice of thanks.

Kasaya Robes

*I was originated in India,
monastics there wore me
during alms offering and
Dharma functions.
Chinese Buddhism came from
India, in this connection,
Chinese had to wear me if they
would like to be a monastic.*

The kasaya, or monastic robes, are a kind of religious attire worn by members of the Buddhist monastic order. The Sanskrit name kasaya is a reference to the faded or stained color appropriate for monastic attire. Kasaya are made by cutting cloth into pieces and sewing them together to resemble a rice field. Because of this the robe is also called futian yi (福田衣), "field of merit robe" or gejie yi (割截衣), "patchwork robe."

Kasaya are also sometimes called cibei fu (慈悲服), "compassion clothes," wushang yi (無上衣), "unsurpassed clothes," lichen fu (離塵服), "renunciation clothes," and jietuo fu (解脫服), "liberation clothes."

There are three types of monastic robes: the great robe, the inner robe, and the upper robe, together called the "triple robe." The inner robe is worn for everyday activities or while doing work. The upper robe is worn when teaching, chanting, or during monastic assemblies. The great robe is worn during formal talks, debates, formal meetings of the monastic order, or meeting dignitaries. The monastic robes are the emblem of Buddhism and the hallmark of the noble ones, how could they not bring great merit? Emperor Shunzhi (r. 1644-1661 CE) of the Qing dynasty composed a verse about the kasaya, exalting monastic life:

> *Gold and jade are not dear,*
> *Only the monsatic's robe is hard to wear.*

I come from the dynasty of the Han, and I am nineteen centuries old. I followed the Indian monastics as they travelled the road to China to propagate the Dharma. During the centuries that I have lived in China, I have suffered some hardships, but my history is mostly a glorious one.

Since I was originated in India, monastics there wore me during alms offering and Dharma functions. Chinese Buddhism came from India and the Chinese had to wear me if they wanted to be monastics.

There are several different kinds of us *kasaya* robes, each with a specific function within the sangha: the *sanghati* or outer robe, the *uttarasanga* or upper robe, and the *anatarvasaka* or lower robe. Since the time of the Buddha, monastics have possessed these three robes and one bowl as their companions. When traveling, they did not have to worry about where to stay or what to eat. I can't even count the number of monastics who have lived their lives with me as a companion.

Through the ages people enjoying the pleasures of this mundane, Saha world would feel pity for monastics when they would see them put on their robes and live the simple life of a monk. They thought that monks must lead a very lonely existence, void of any of the enjoyments of life. But Emperor Shunzhi[15] put that foolish notion to rest. When the emperor realized the difficulty of being a monastic—that one must have the proper causes and conditions—he realized that the value of gold and white jade paled in comparison to the value of the monastic who wears the robe.

I remember that Sakyamuni Buddha said that those who take refuge as his followers would not starve as long as they had their robes with them. Have you seen any practicing monastics who were suffering from hunger? In China today, many monastics, lacking the resolve to live the monastic life, willingly take off their robes and re-enter the mundane world of struggle and suffering. If I could, I would try to dissuade them from going back to a world consumed by the three poisons of greed, anger, and ignorance, where the strong bully the weak and people are always in conflict with one another. Only in Buddhism can one find some light and purity in the darkness of the Saha world.

I don't disapprove of all monastics who take off their robes. Today, many patriotic monks, who are practitioners of Mahayana Buddhism, have taken off their *kasaya* robes and put on the uniform of the armed forces. I admire them for following this path. However, some monks, when they take off their robes, wear western suits and eat fish and meat. They no longer practice or preach the Dharma and no longer take refuge in the Buddha. It saddens me to think that these ungrateful people do not appreciate the gift of the Triple Gem. Unfortunately, there are also some cases where monastics will wear the triple robe, but will not follow the Dharma or take refuge in the Buddha.

Some people are envious because they hold the mistaken view that monastics live a life of leisure, free from duties and responsibilities. However, when these people study Buddhism, they realize that monastics work very hard fulfilling their responsibilities of personal cultivation, teaching the Dharma, and working to liberate all sentient beings. Some lay people feel that they have many duties and responsibilities, but when they became monastics, they find that they are busier than ever. If you're not willing to accept

the responsibility of working to liberate all sentient beings, you should not aspire to become a "sangha jewel." Another name for a sangha jewel is "field of merit." This is why *kasaya* robes are called "field of merit robes," because when donning the robe, the monastic allows all living beings to cultivate merits. It is neither simple nor easy to be a monastic. But if you cannot lead and inspire others through example—by living a virtuous life and strictly following the precepts—then you should not put on the robes.

In the past, I have been used in much the same way as a medal is used today: as a symbol for honoring and recognizing a person's outstanding or meritorious service and contribution to society. In ancient times, an emperor would present a monk with a *kasaya* robe when the monk was given the title of National Master. During the reign of Empress Wu Zetian[16] of the Tang dynasty, Master Falang and eight other monastics were given purple robes in honor of their accomplishments in translating the *Great Cloud Sutra*. Their work had a significant impact on Chinese history and Buddhist culture.

In the past, people could wear me with a feeling of pride, and they were treated with respect by society. Nowadays, when monastics wear the *kasaya*, they are scoffed at and ridiculed as being superstitious or old fashioned. This tragic state of affairs is a sad result of some monastics not being faithful to their precepts and giving all monastics a bad name. These unfaithful monastics have brought shame and dishonor to me and to Buddhism, as well.

Originally, I was not worn when prostrating before gods, ghosts, sprits of the dead, or parents. But as time went on, monastics presiding at funeral services wearing red and green *kasaya* robes would kneel down and talk to the spirits of the deceased. Sometimes these same monastics would place images of gods, little ghosts, or guardians of hell on the altar and kneel down to offer prayers. By not faithfully following the rules for Buddhist monastics, they not only brought dishonor to themselves but they sullied my reputation, too.

Not only were there rules regarding behavior for monastics when they wore the *kasaya*, there were also regulations regarding robes for monastics and robes for the laity. Lay followers who took the five precepts wore the *lichan* robe (禮懺衣),[17] and monastics who took the bodhisattva vows wore the *uttarasanga* robe. Nowadays, it seems as though anyone with a shaven head can wear me. No one asks or seems to care about whether or not someone has actually taken the precepts, and whether or not they should be wearing a robe for lay followers or a robe for monastics. Ritual and tradition represent the spirit of Buddhism, and I think I have lost my dignity. Can anyone still respect me?

I am ashamed to say that you will see many strange things these days. Lay women with curly hair are conducting funeral services, and lay men with Western-style haircuts and wearing red *sanghati* robes are officiating at Yogacara Flaming Mouth ceremonies.

Some monastics officiating at funeral services use still another piece of clothing called a "red water" robe. During the service, they wear this robe and are followed by the coffin and a band that plays to attract spectators to the service. Society laughs at this spectacle and looks down upon me. Now, even monks who are expounding the sutras and wearing the red *sanghati* robes are laughed at. I am considered to be out dated and old fashioned. I have had a proud and noble history, but I have fallen on disastrous times. How can I resolve this tragic state of affairs?

Meditation Stick

I am shaped like a "treasure" sword—
a valuable and finely crafted sword
used by heroes and warriors
in China since antiquity.
Respect for and observation
of precepts and regulations are
basic to monastic life.
I am used as the enforcer.

Originating in the Chan School of Buddhism, the meditation stick (xiangban) is a wooden paddle shaped like a sword that is used to deliver a warning stroke to practitioners. Its purpose is to maintain discipline and order within the Buddhist monastic community.

Meditation sticks have various names depending on their function. A "warning stick" is used as a warning to remind practitioners to put forth effort in their cultivation. A "law stick" is used to punish those who break the monastic precepts. A "patrol stick" is used to awaken those who are sleeping or distracted during sitting meditation. A "supervisory stick" is used to monitor extended meditation retreats. In general, the meditation stick is wielded by such monastic officers as the abbot, meditation session chief, meditation elder, meditation session advisor, hall director, or discipline master.

They call me the meditation stick. If you've ever come to a temple or lived in a monastery, you know that I'm used for hitting people. Just the mention of these two words in the same sentence—hitting and people—causes everybody to be wary of me and keep their distance. And it's exactly because of the way people feel about me that I have been used for the past several hundred years to maintain discipline and ensure that the precepts and regulations are followed by Buddhist monastics.

Respect for the law is fundamental to the orderly functioning of a country. If people break the law, then there are penalties imposed. Depending upon the seriousness of the crime, punishment can range from fines to imprisonment and even death. Similarly, respect for and observation of precepts and regulations are basic to monastic life. I am used as the enforcer.

I am shaped like a "treasure" sword—a valuable and finely crafted sword used by heroes and warriors in China since antiquity. The story of how I came to be shaped as I am and used in Buddhist monasteries is a fascinating one! During the reign of Emperor Kangxi,[18] there lived an eminent monk, National Master[19] Yulin. At the time when Yongzheng followed Kangxi as the next emperor, Master Yulin had already entered *nirvana*. Emperor Yongzheng greatly admired Master Yulin, so he issued a proclamation proclaiming his appreciation for the master's contributions, to both China and Buddhism. The emperor decided to locate any of Master Yulin's disciples.

One monk, with a head grotesquely covered in scabies pustules, came forward, claiming to have been a disciple of Master

Yulin at Gaomin Temple. He said that his abbot had sent him to the capital to gain an audience with the emperor. Emperor Yongzheng, a serious practitioner of Chan Buddhism, spoke with the monk and immediately realized that he had only a shallow understanding of Chan. Outraged by such dishonor to the name and memory of Master Yulin, the emperor ordered a special meditation room set up in the palace. There the monk was ensconced and told that he had just seven days to attain enlightenment. If at the end of the seven days, he had not attained enlightenment, a treasure sword, which was hanging on the wall in the front of the room, would be used to behead him.

At the end of seven days, the scabies infested monk had not attained enlightenment, but the monk asked the attendant guarding the meditation chamber to make a request to the emperor for another seven days. The emperor granted a stay of one week. However, on the sixth day of the stay, the monk was still unenlightened. The attendant said to him, "You mangy monk! You imposter! You false disciple of National Master Yulin! Tomorrow's the last day. If you haven't attained enlightenment, the emperor will use that treasure sword to take off your head!"

Upon hearing the attendant's words, the monk suddenly attained enlightenment. He shouted, "Bring me the treasure sword. I'll take off the emperor's head!" The attendant thought the poor fellow had gone crazy and rushed to report this turn of events to the emperor. When the emperor heard the report, he knew immediately what had happened.

The admonitions of the attendant and threat of the emperor using the sword had helped to bring about the causes and conditions necessary for the monk to attain enlightenment. The monk was honored in recognition of his attainment. After news of what had taken place spread, Chan temples and monasteries began using wooden meditation sticks shaped like treasure swords to encourage and admonish their own monastics.

Since that time, while my shape has not changed, my use has become widespread. Now, there are various meditation sticks used for different purposes. The "warning stick" can be used at any time; the "law stick" is used when a monk has violated rules; and the "patrol stick" is used to startle or awaken monastics when they fall asleep or lose concentration during meditation. Each meditation stick is inscribed with its special function.

Generally, the meditation stick is used when people have violated the rules. But even when there has been no transgression, a master might hit a practitioner at any time in the meditation hall. There is an old saying regarding this practice that goes, "The first hit can eliminate bad karma, the second can bring wisdom, and the third can bring enlightenment." People believe that there are benefits to being hit by the meditation stick. In fact, one time, a famous woman presented an old monk with a donation of several thousand *yuan* along with her request that she be hit by the meditation stick. When this happened, I felt that my integrity was being compromised, because it seemed as if the monk was accepting a bribe for using me.

There was a limitation on my use. I could only be used by a fully-ordained monastic. These days, in some places, you would be hard-pressed even to find me. Even if you could find me, you would find very few qualified monastics. It is sad to see how membership in the sangha has declined.

Meditation sticks are used most frequently in reception, chanting, and meditation halls. The discipline master would order the monastic to kneel down to be struck by the meditation stick. I was very visible at sangha food offerings and at precepts retreats. Senior monks walked around carrying me, looking like soldiers carrying swords. As you can imagine, there was not much talking or looking around at these affairs.

Unfortunately, the use of the meditation stick in monastic life was sometimes excessive, abusive, and arbitrary. Just as feudal lords were known to cruelly torture people sometimes, some of the monastics in positions of authority would use me to beat other monks and nuns excessively because of personal dislike or petty disagreements. Infatuated with their power, they would show off in front of novice monastics. How tragic were these poisonous actions of the Saha world to the life of Buddhist monasteries.

In civil society, everyone from the highest official to the ordinary citizen should be held accountable for following the law. The same principle should apply to monastic life; however, in some monasteries, abbots and other monastics in positions of authority have not been held to the same standard of discipline as ordinary monks and nuns. Monastic reformers—wanting to eliminate these abuses—proclaimed that I was an instrument used by the powerful to oppress the powerless.

The saddest sight to see was a monastic who had been severely punished, being turned out of the monastery after being beaten by the meditation stick. My heart would ache to see a monk, weak from a beating, forced by a monastic official to pack up his few belongings and leave the monastery. I was not proud of myself at times like these. Where was the compassion in all this? I wanted to denounce these disgraceful monks before the statue of the Buddha.

In addition to me, willow twigs and rattan sticks have been used as tools of discipline in monasteries. Monastics were not allowed to cry out while being struck or to sob afterwards. They had to bow and prostrate to the person who beat them and promise to repent. As Western ideas of democracy gradually spread to China, their influence was felt in Buddhist monasteries. Consequently, disciplining with the meditation stick came to be regarded as a barbaric practice. However, I know that what was being rejected was not me; it was the abuses of the system that I'm sorry to have had to describe to you.

Just as the meditation stick was used in monasteries for discipline and punishment, so was the ruler used in schools. In monasteries, monastics were hit on the shoulder with the meditation stick, and in schools students were hit on the palms of their hands with the ruler. The government has since prohibited the use of rulers for corporal punishment in public schools. While no one has outlawed the use of the meditation stick in monasteries, I want to share my thoughts on the subject.

While the use of the meditations stick has a long tradition, rules regarding its use have to be applied fairly and equally to all, whether they are abbots or the least senior of monks. I should not be used for minor rule infractions, and I should be used to strike only the shoulders of monastics. I should only be used to discipline those who do not work to proclaim the Dharma for the sake of all sentient beings, and, instead, invest money for personal gain. Used for those who do not practice the precepts, and, instead, make money performing funeral services. And last but not least, used for those who do not follow the Dharma, and, instead, criticize others and manipulate their positions for their own purposes. These are the monastics most in need of correction.

Monastic Shoes

Why there is a split down the front?
We are made this way as
an implication of awareness.
Whenever the monastic
looks down at me,
it is an everlasting reminder
of the impermanence of
all phenomena.

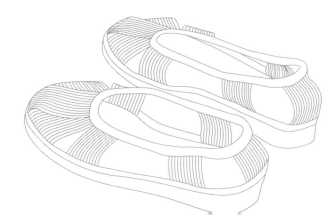

Also called arhat shoes, monastic shoes come in muted colors like grey, black, and brown. They are designed with a total of six openings along the front, back, and sides of the shoes. These six openings exhort monastics to "lower their heads and see through illusion," as they travel through their day. Monastics must see through the illusion of the six sense organs of eyes, ears, nose, tongue, body, and mind, the six sense objects of sight, sound, smell, taste, touch, and dharmas, the six realms of existence of heaven, asuras, human beings, animals, hungry ghosts, and hell, and the six great afflictions of greed, anger, ignorance, pride, doubt, and false views. Monastics must also see through the brevity and insignificance of life.

The six openings around each shoe also remind monastics to cultivate the six perfections of giving, morality, patience, diligence, meditative concentration, and prajna in each step, and to remember the six points of reverent harmony: maintain physical harmony by living together, maintain verbal harmony by avoiding disputes, maintain mental harmony by sharing happiness, maintain harmony in the precepts by practicing together, maintain harmony of view by sharing the same understanding, and maintain economic harmony by sharing equally.

F ashionably dressed ladies wear high-heel pumps, muscle-bound sportsmen wear athletic footgear, and monks and nuns wear monastic shoes. Shoes come in an assortment of styles for a diverse range of people and purposes. Today, I, a pair of monastic shoes, would like to talk to you about my family background, as well as describe for you some notable events that have occurred in my lifetime.

It sure has been rueful with terrible suffering . The reason for my misery is that men and women, both young and old, have discarded traditional Chinese-style cloth shoes in favor of Western-style leather footwear. Examining the current scene, it appears that my fortune is cut from the same fabric as the traditional cloth shoes. Have you noticed that I'm gradually being seen less and less on the feet of monastics?

In the past, many large towns had stores for purchasing monastic shoes. However, probably influenced by the changing new trends, monastics nowadays are buying fewer monastic shoes. Sadly, these specialty stores have had to close their doors. But just like the decorous figures of old, there are still a few monastics who are willing to preserve whatever traditions are left in Buddhism, just like those people who preserve the customs of their country. Wishing not to be influenced by modern vogue, they have their monastic shoes custom made. I am very grateful to them.

Monastic shoes come in several different designs. There are "climbing tiger" shoes, yellow monastic shoes, and *arhat* shoes. *Arhat* shoes were originally woven from straw, but now they are sewn from cloth. The ancient patriarchs had many stories to tell about us. The climbing tiger and yellow monastic shoes have a split down the front with three strands woven together. Do you know why there is a split down the front? We are made this way as an implication of awareness. Whenever the monastic looks down at me, it is an everlasting reminder of the impermanence of all phenomena. *Arhat* shoes are also called straw shoes because that is what they were originally made of. But in this world continuously undergoing alterations, *arhat* shoes have gone through phases of being made from ramie, cloth, and, eventually, even leather. With the course things are taking, it even seems possible that one of these days, monastics will be wearing shoes made of glass!

Monastic shoes would experience quite extraordinary wear, because monastics would often tour widely. They were said to travel about land the way the clouds swim across the sky. I felt fortunate that the monastics wore me on so many journeys, because I was able to see many scenic sights and visit many venerable masters. Many monastics gained knowledge and a deeper understanding of Dharma practice as they traveled. When that happened, they would be happy and say, "I haven't wasted money by putting such wear on my straw shoes." If they decided that travel was unnecessary, they would say, "I have saved money by not using my straw shoes." I appreciated and admired these monastics. Although they wandered the world as weeds drifting upon water, they were disciplined and well behaved, and I felt safe and secure with them. They would undertake long and dangerous paths seeking teachings from numerous eminent patriarchs and renowned masters in hopes of freeing themselves from the cycle of birth and death. When their efforts were unsuccessful, they would sigh with dismay and say, "I have worn out my straw shoes, but I'm still not enlightened!"

Just like the sighing of these monastics, who traveled around and visited so many masters in hopes of liberation from birth and death, I, too, carry a lot of sadness inside of me. Whenever the monastics traveled far and wide and still did not find what they were looking for, time slowly marched onward, the road stretched longer and longer, and thread by thread the last of my strength and stamina unraveled. When this happened, we monastic shoes were worn out. Still even then, some monastics refused to discard us, faithfully carrying us with them. But other monastics—mindful of the emptiness and impermanence of all things—instead, ditched us by the side of the road. I know I shouldn't accuse these monks of being cruel and indifferent, but it is unbelievable that, after I have dedicated my entire life to serving my master, I am simply to be cast off when old and worn out! It is a hard thing to accept when my road ends in abandonment, cruelly exposed to the harsh rain and wind.

Oh, but there are so many moving stories about me. In Buddhism, when devotees want to make offerings to a monastic, they will often use monastic shoes. There is one story about Master Lianchi after he had left home to become a monk. His wife, who was still a layperson, made a pair of shoes for him, but fearing ensnaring attachments and not wanting to be bound by his wife's love, he came to a bold decision. He sliced me in half! Although I suffered from some temporary pain, I still admired Master Lianchi's fierce devotion to his Dharma practice. If you don't believe me, here is a poem written by Master Lianchi to declare what he had done.

My wife in my lay life sent me one pair of shoes
Sewn with 10,000 needles and strands of thread;

One sword severing the red silken line,[20]
From now on, I will not bear any dust.

Cultivating the Dharma needs this kind of determination. Without it how can anyone enter the Buddha's path?

Here is another touching yet tragic story that took place around 1930. There was a master who thought that Buddhism had ceased having importance in the daily lives of people because of a failure to develop a system of Buddhist education. He vowed that all the money he raised from almsgiving would be used for establishing educational programs. However, some benefactors, who did not realize the value of Buddhist education, were reluctant to donate generously. Instead, they wanted their money to be used for other projects, such as temple restoration and supporting people who did nothing, or waiting for others to occupy the place. To call attention to what he was trying to accomplish, this master would stand on nails all day and night, neither eating nor sitting down. After several days of following this regime, he passed away. When his disciples heard of his demise, they raced to the spot, only to find that their master had already been cremated. Only his monastic shoes remained. Later, his disciples built a house, where I was placed on display in honor of his memory. How I respect such people, but it is sad to think that even the sacrifice of this master failed to awaken some stubborn devotees to the need for Buddhist education. This gives me such a sharp stabbing pain in my heart.

I urge you not to scoff at the power of monastic shoes. Master Jigong had a pair of worn out shoes that was his magic weapon. Whenever he was unable to avoid a fight or being bullied by people, he would take off his shoes. One time when he was being taunted and insulted, he decided not to argue with the tormentors.

Instead, he stepped out of his shoes and chanted, "*om mani padme hum*." The shoes suddenly jumped up and started defending Jigong. Here is a warning to everyone! Monastics cannot be insulted with impunity! You should listen to my advice, or watch out for the superpowers of monastic shoes.

I remember one other occasion when a monk suddenly lost one of his shoes. He searched everywhere, but no matter what, he failed to find the missing shoe. He just couldn't believe that a thief had taken it. Why would anyone steal just one shoe?

Several years later, a beautiful woman made a pair of shoes and sent them to the monk. The monk did not understand why this woman should give him such a gift. It was some time after this that he finally found out what had happened to his shoe. The woman had been married for many years, but was unable to have a child. She heard a story somewhere that claimed that, if a woman were to steal the shoe of a monastic and put the shoe into a chest, a son would be born to her. After hearing this story, she had taken the monastic's shoe. She followed this practice, and, sure enough, she gave birth to a son. The new pair of shoes that she sent to the monk was to show her gratitude. I thought it a huge joke that people held this strange belief that I was some kind of a bodhisattva who could give people sons! Do people really believe that I have some influence on the business of having babies? They must think that I am Guanyin Bodhisattva, who brings children. Oh, great compassionate Guanyin Bodhisattva!

The countenance of monks and nuns with their robes, shaven heads, and monastic shoes is so dignified. But nowadays, many monastics disdain such apparel like me; instead, they wear wooden-soled clogs when walking around statues of the Buddha and chanting in the shrine. You can imagine the noise those wooden soles on those clogs adds during walking meditation—the *ding-ding-ding* of the hand bell, the *knock-knock-knock* of the wooden fish, and then that *clip-clop clip-clop* noise of those wooden shoes. How can the meditators possibly feel solemn and respectful! Contrast, if you will, the attitude of these modern monastics with that of Bodhidharma, the first Chan patriarch. It is said that Bodhidharma revered his monastic shoes so much that he took one shoe with him and returned to India upon his death.

Alms Bowl

*During the Golden Age of
Chinese Buddhism,
bowls were not used just for
begging and eating.
Both the kasaya robe and I
were used as symbols of
Dharma transmission.*

An alms bowl is a round, oval-shaped eating vessel used by monastics, with a flat bottom and a narrowed opening with which they receive offerings from human and heavenly beings. Its composition and size is described in the monastic rules, so that it holds the appropriate amount of food for the stomach. The rules stipulate that an alms bowl must be crude in form to not create greed, dark grey in color to not incite desire, and of a fixed size to encourage contentment.

Originally, having an alms bowl was an everyday necessity, but as Buddhism was transmitted to China the practice of making daily food offerings was not adopted by the Chinese laity. However, as stipulated in the monastic rules, alms bowls are still given when a monastic is ordained, though few actually use their bowl. The alms bowl still stands as an emblem of how all Buddhas, as numerous as grains of sand in the Ganges, practiced to end their desire. All those who receive the alms bowl should focus their mind to act with self-control and self-respect.

My name is *patra* in Sanskrit and *yingliang qi* in Chinese. In English, I'm called an alms bowl. In the early days of Buddhism, Sakyamuni Buddha and his disciples used me to obtain their food. They would go out with their alms bowls to get food for their daily meal. In ancient China, monks and nuns couldn't get along without me. Even though there was enough to eat in the monastery, members of the community were not given any food without having their bowls. That is why monastics with their bowls were said to be exactly like clouds floating in the sky, for they did not need to worry about where their food would come from. It was said, "One bowl has held the food of a thousand families. A solitary monastic travels on his journey of a hundred thousand miles seeking liberation from the cycle of birth and death."

In those early days of Buddhism, monks and nuns would take their bowls and go out begging for food. But over time the sangha became more established. Monasteries farmed or leased their own land, generating their own revenue. Monastics did not have to beg for the necessities of life, and, eventually, I was no longer used.

Chinese Buddhism originated, so to speak, from the practice of begging for food. But it then became self-sustaining by maintaining properties. The monasteries without properties had to generate income by accepting donations and offering to chant sutras and other Dharma services. This change from begging for food to managing land and properties and engaging in other enterprises to raise money has led to confusion about Buddhism in the minds of many people.

During the Golden Age of Chinese Buddhism, bowls were not used just for begging and eating. Both the *kasaya* robe and I were used as symbols of Dharma transmission. A patriarch—familiar with the dedication, understanding of the Dharma, and education of his disciples—would choose his successor. As a symbol, the patriarch would pass down his robe and bowl to the next patriarch. Through this transmission, the new patriarch vowed to continue the noble task of liberating all sentient beings. Sakyamuni Buddha passed down his robe and bowl to Mahakasyapa. It was Bodhidharma, the twenty-eighth Indian patriarch, who brought Chan Buddhism to China, along with his robe and bowl.

After the fifth Chinese patriarch, Hongren, named Huineng[21] as his successor, he asked Huineng to take his bowl and robe and travel to southern China. The Fifth Patriarch made this request because he knew his selection of Huineng as the Sixth Patriarch would be controversial. He wanted Huineng to leave until the matter was resolved. Huineng, taking his bowl and robe, followed Master Hongren's request and traveled south.

One of Hongren's other disciples, a monk named Huiming, had been a famous general as a layperson. He was upset when he heard about what was happening, and he pursued Huineng. He planned to take the robe and bowl away from him. When Huiming was just about to overtake the Sixth Patriarch, Huineng quickly set me down and hid himself behind a bush. Huiming approached me and tried to pick me up. Then a strange thing happened. No matter how hard he tried, Huiming could not pick me up. Humbled, Huiming said, "Master, I'm here for the Dharma, not for the alms bowl." Master Huineng then revealed himself and preached the Dharma

to Huiming, who, thereupon, obtained enlightenment. Although I am only a small alms bowl, you can see that I have played an important role in the transmission of the Dharma.

Here are some interesting observations about begging for food. Mahakasyapa never begged for food from the rich, only from the poor. He believed that giving the poor an opportunity to give alms was a blessing to them. Subhuti took the opposite view. He begged for food from the rich because he did not want to burden the poor. The Buddha had stated that true mind does not discriminate, and, consequently it is not right to limit the begging from either the poor or the rich. Ananda begged food from everyone. However, he was endangered by a woman named Matangi.[22]

I was involved in the suffering and death of some people when I was in Maudgalyayana's hands. Prince Virudhaka, the son of King Prasenajit of Kosala, had a personal grudge against the Sakya people and wanted to wipe out the entire clan. Maudgalyayana implored the Buddha to save these people, but the Buddha replied that he was powerless to change the Sakya people's karma. Even so, Maudgalyayana was certain that something could be done. He used his supernatural powers to hide five hundred people from the Sakya clan in his bowl and sent them up to the heavens. When the slaughter was over, and the carnage assessed, even the Sakyans Maudgalyayana had tried to save had turned into blood. It was just as the Buddha had said. A person cannot save another from the karma that they have created. Good seeds produce good fruit, and bad seeds produce bad fruit. A small bowl like me could not save them!

In China, there is a famous legend that tells the story of how Chan Master Fahai subjugated a powerful white snake that appeared in the form of a woman. Though the snake was big and powerful, she was shrunk down to the size of an alms bowl, becoming just a small, weak creature. It is said that this legend grew from the story of Sakyamuni Buddha conquering the fire dragon using his alms bowl. From this story, you can see that besides being used for food, I have also been used to conquer demons!

In the past, some monks and nuns treasured their precious bowls. They would give up everything else except for their bowl and robe. Here is a story regarding Chan Master Jin Bifong, who, even after he had cleared his mind and seen his true nature, continued to treasure his jade begging bowl. At the time of this story, the master had lived his allotted number of years, and the King of Hell wanted him. On several occasions, the ruler of the underworld had already ordered little ghosts to catch Master Jin Bifong. However, each time that they tried, the master was in *samadhi*, a state of deep meditative concentration, and the ghosts could not reach him. The King of Hell became angry.

The earth god, upon hearing about this, suggested to the ghosts that, since the master was so attached to his jade bowl, they could trick him by shaking his bowl. Upon hearing the noise, Master Jin Bifong would come out of *samadhi*, and the ghosts would be able to catch him. The ghosts decided to carry out this plan according to the earth god's advice.

When the master heard the noise coming from his precious jade bowl, he left *samadhi*. Opening his eyes and seeing the ghosts with iron chains, he realized what was happening. At that moment, he was able to free himself from the chains of greed and attachment, and he smashed the jade bowl to the ground. He told the ghosts to give him a few moments, and then he again entered into *samadhi*. In that meditative concentration, he spoke to the little ghosts: "If you want to capture Jin Bifong, you will need chains that can bind emptiness. If you can't contain emptiness, then you can't catch Jin Bifong." Here, I want to remind all monastics that they should free themselves of the poison of greed, even when it comes to their begging bowls.

Even after Master Jin Bifong's experience, people still have remained attached to me.

The monk Su Manshu, who was also a poet, would not give me up, even during the most difficult time of his life. When nothing seemed to be going right and he was living in poverty, he wrote this poem about me.

> With worn out shoes and broken bowl,
> This unknown wanderer has crossed many
>   bridges
> and seen the cherry blossoms through many
>   seasons.

From these sentiments, we can see how attached he was to his bowl.

Theravada Buddhism[23] has kept up the tradition of begging for food to this day. I hear people discussing the pros and cons of begging for food by members of the sangha. Those in favor claim that when holding their bowls and begging for food, monks and nuns are more accessible to ordinary citizens. Consequently, it is easier to explain and propagate the Dharma. Proponents claim an additional advantage of begging is that it is an excellent discipline to subjugate the false sense of self and practice humility.

Those opposed to the practice claim that begging for food is not a good idea, because some people might view members of the sangha as being lazy, living off the labor of others. I have found the arguments of both sides to be very persuasive and cannot decide one way or the other.

In Chinese Buddhism nowadays, I am not used much except for taking meals during ordinations. In Taiwan, there are monastics who may have never seen me. Since I am made from porcelain, I am sometimes called a "porcelain bowl." During retreats, the monk in charge will ask those on retreat whether they want an iron bowl or a porcelain bowl. Anyone who does not reply with the words "porcelain bowl" is not allowed to take the precepts. Why is it, then, that today's monastics have no special feeling for me?

Sutra Cabinet

*If we sutra cabinets
weren't here to make sure
the sutras stayed organized and safe,
then who would keep the
Buddha's teachings and
all these commentaries and
devotional writings of the patriarchs
and sages from getting lost?*

A sutra cabinet is where the sutras, the written teachings of Buddhism, are stored. The sutras were compiled by a council of the Buddha's disciples following his final nirvana in order to ensure that the Buddha's teachings would long endure in the world. A total of five hundred arhats attended this council, and from among these, two representatives were chosen: the Venerable Ananda, known as the foremost in hearing, presided over the collection of teachings (sutra), and the Venerable Upali, known as the foremost in knowledge of the monastic rules, presided over the collection of rules (vinaya).

Ananda was the Buddha's attendant and was always at his side. His memory was astonishing, for he was able to accurately and unerringly retain in his memory the circumstances and content of each and every teaching of the Buddha that he heard. When the teachings were being compiled it was Ananda who recited from memory, one after another, the previous teachings given by the Buddha. Then the great arhats would examine and approve the teachings, and later confirm them when there were no longer any objections. The sutras are the written records of this council, preserving not only the oral teachings of the Buddha, but also his teachings by example.

W hen they made me, they nailed boards together and painted me red. I'm something that holds books. I've been put here in this big, tall building with lots of stories. It's a storehouse for all the precious pages of these Buddhist sutras. I get to be on the highest floor of the whole temple. I'm really proud to be called "sutra cabinet," even if I'm not exactly your regular run of the mill cabinet or bookcase. I may not be an expensive object, but I'm used to store priceless treasures—the original sutras written on palm leaves and the Tripitaka, to name just two. There are nine thousand fascicles of the Buddhist sutras! If we sutra cabinets weren't here to make sure they stayed organized and safe, then who would keep the Buddha's teachings and all these commentaries and devotional writings of the patriarchs and sages from getting lost?

I think about how after the Buddha became enlightened, he spent forty-nine years preaching in hopes that the wonderful Dharma would reach the hearts of all sentient beings. Since then, there have been three major times when followers have come together as one big group to collect and organize the Buddha's teachings. And in my country, many eminent monks have made long, difficult, and dangerous journeys to India to get and bring back written copies of the sutras and other early Buddhist writings. Today, several thousand of the fascicles make up the Taisho Tripitaka. This is one that is entrusted to my care. In the early centuries of Chinese Buddhism, the job of translating and interpreting the Buddhist scriptures was a high-priority project. It even had support from the emperor! During this time, every single translation that was made of each sutra was meticulously inspected for accuracy by thousands of very learned monastics. The work of translating the sutras that's being done today, even by the National Institute for Translation and Compilation, pales in comparison to the number of translations that were produced during the Golden Age of Chinese Buddhism.

The sacred teachings of Buddhism are organized into four divisions. The first division is the sutras themselves. These are the recorded teachings of Sakyamuni Buddha. The second division is called the *vinaya*. This has the monastic code of discipline that was laid down by Sakyamuni Buddha. Next is the Abhidharma. These are commentaries on what's in the first two divisions. The fourth division is made up of miscellaneous writings. Some of the scriptures are said to be down right great literature. They also talk about a lot of different subjects—like science and philosophy. The whole collection of Buddhist scriptures describes in minute detail the universal conditions and origins of the various worlds that sentient beings are reborn into during the cycle of birth and death.

Over the centuries, the treasures on my shelves have had a big effect on the culture, morals, and politics of China. Their value has also spread to other cultures and countries. Westerners also have been exploring the riches of the Tripitaka. Recently, while stationed in Japan, many American soldiers have discovered and taken an interest in the collection of sutras and commentary called the *Taisho Tripitaka*.[24]

It's too bad that some people look down upon the sutras. Since these people usually don't put in the time and effort to understand my treasures, when they try to talk about them, all that comes out is just a bunch of blathering buzz. I truly feel sorry for the people

who put down the Dharma teachings. Without the sutras on my shelves, how are they ever going to find the meaning of life in this Saha world?

Many scientists, philosophers and scholars have found wisdom and inspiration from the pages I protect. For example, Wang Xiaoxu and You Zhibiao[25] both furnished science with important contributions after they had studied the sutras. Albert Einstein came to China and studied the sutras while he was working on his Theory of Relativity. Then there was the famous French philosopher who made a vow to become a monk after reading the sutras. A well-known man of letters once chose the *Lotus Sutra* as the subject of his doctoral dissertation. In China, Professors Liang Qichao and Hu Shizhi, who taught classes on Chinese history and culture, made their students read the actual sutras and also the commentaries by the eminent Buddhist masters because of the contributions these writings have made to the Chinese way of thinking. Many people who want to understand the mysteries of life and the universe partake of the treasures of the sutra cabinet!

The Dharma teachings I hold fast on my shelves are so profound that monastics who wanted to teach the Dharma would spend years in study and preparation. But I've never looked kindly upon those who've used the sutra cabinet only for finding and memorizing commentaries on the sutras that they could use in their Dharma talks. What Buddhism needs are monks and nuns who express their own thoughts and understandings of the Dharma! After all, the commentaries are the thoughts and reflections of other monastics that have studied and reflected on the Buddha's teachings. If monks and nuns don't delve deeply into the profound truths of the sutras themselves, then how will they be able to preach the Dharma very well! The Dharma is very profound and not always easily understood by the average layperson. And the meanings of the words and way they're used have changed over the centuries. That's why we need Dharma teachers who can present the Dharma in a way that the average person can understand.

I'm sad when I see the way most people are living their lives today. They're not interested in studying the Dharma or in cultivating themselves. Instead, they just go after creature comforts and nice clothing. They waste their time spreading idle gossip and harmful rumors. How sad to see their lives rotting away like that!

During those first centuries of Chinese Buddhism, as the number of volumes in sutra cabinets increased from all those sutras that were translated and the many commentaries that were written, people were invited to come to study and read them. Unfortunately, many monasteries and temples don't allow open access to the sutras anymore, because they're afraid that the pages might get damaged. I think it's shameful that the abbots in these monasteries and temples aren't contributing anything themselves to people's understanding of the Dharma. Their policies are just making it hard for people to know about the Dharma.

I have a complaint to file about being kept imprisoned in this pagoda where my sutras are slowly being eaten by worms. During the rainy season, I'm surrounded by moisture and the rank odor of mildew. I feel like boring, old, dead wood being locked away in this monastery. Somebody bust me out of here and take me to a public library, where people can read the Buddhist scriptures again! If I can't make the Dharma available to the public, people will start to get the wrong idea about Buddhism and think that it's about secret occult teachings or something.

Here's another bug that's crawled into my knothole. Sometimes the members from the unorthodox sects, who pretend to be true Buddhists, place books on my shelves that are not true to the Dharma. Since people who aren't serious practitioners can't tell which books have the true Dharma, I urge all the masters and monastics who are dedicated to the true teachings to clean everything out of the sutra cabinets that's not actually a part of the treasury of Buddhist scripture. If someone would do this, then I could concentrate on doing my job of housing and protecting the Dharma jewel. You know, the Dharma jewel is just like a compass that points the way for sentient beings to have a peaceful, happy life and a bright future.

Pagoda

The reason I can be called "pagoda"
is because of my close relationship
with the Triple Gem, that is,
the Buddha, the Dharma,
and the Sangha.
During the early years of Buddhism,
pagodas were built to provide
a place to house and venerate
the relics of the Buddha.

A pagoda is a more highly decorated version of the Indic stupa, a burial mound within which is placed a reliquary jar. Two hundred years after the Buddha's final nirvana, there appeared in India a great ruler by the name of King Asoka who unified the whole country and was a great patron of Buddhism. During his reign he built eighty-four thousand stupas all over his kingdom, and since then the stupa has become a way for Buddhists to remember the Buddha by paying homage to his relics.

As Buddhism spread to different countries and cultures, the stupa was adapted to various architectural styles. Some stupas are grand and imposing, some are dignified and immaculately white, while some are classically simple and elegant. They can be dome-shaped, have one or more terraces, or be built in the spire-like Tibetan style, and consist of three main parts: the base, the body, and the top, which usually terminates in an ornamental finial.

Photograph by Ven. Hui Rong

If you have taken a close look at Buddhist temples lately, you surely would have noticed that the construction of *me* is the most popular project in all the monasteries today. You can observe across China that both large and small monasteries are busy building me. Abbots, who were once enthusiastic about erecting temples, have now suddenly changed to building me instead. I guess it is an undeniable fact that I am a clever way to cope with the current financial facts of life. Pagoda is my name.

Ever since the Buddha's *parinirvana*, patriarchs and abbots of the past dynasties have built countless numbers of pagodas, but their intentions for building us in those days were quite different from today. During the early years of Buddhism, pagodas were built to provide a place to house and venerate the relics of the Buddha and, later on, the patriarchs who followed. Nowadays we pagodas are built as a source of income for the temples by providing niches in which people can place the ashes of their deceased family members. The reason I can be called "pagoda" is because of my close relationship with the Triple Gem, that is, the Buddha, the Dharma, and the Sangha. But if you took a good look at me today, you would see that I have already lost the true meaning of "gem."

For the past few decades, the economy of Buddhism has been teetering precariously on the verge of collapse. Because of governmental land reform measures, monasteries have lost their landholdings that, in the past, had been able to generate income for them. Many monasteries that had for centuries operated farms for self-sufficiency have been turning to me as a major source of income. Thus, the popularity of pagodas as a means of generating revenues has seen a dramatic increase. The prevailing attitude appears to be that, once you have one of me at your monastery, your existence is guaranteed, because you can fill your coffers with all the money you make off of the dead.

It takes between one hundred thousand to one million *yuan* to build each one of us, and we are being slapped up too quickly. It is sad to see this! Numerous educational institutions, cultural, business, and Buddhist charity organizations are crying out for support from sympathetic people. But few people seem to care and to be willing to lend their aid to these worthy causes. Many of these projects must be discontinued, and some never even get off the ground due to lack of support. But as soon as people hear that there is a project for repairing the pagodas, they immediately start throwing money that way. How selfish people are! They do not really care about other sangha members. All they care about is earning merits for themselves. This is just plain ignorant! They do not realize that merits should be earned by providing benefits to all sentient beings—especially the living ones!

I do not want my life to be extended when I have been built for selfish reasons. There is a saying that goes, "Saving one human life is worth more than building a seven-story pagoda." I fervently wish that people would be involved more in Buddhist endeavors and the activities of sentient beings that benefit the living. Do not always give your attention to the dead.

The building of pagodas began in India with Anathapindika and in China with Master Kang Senghui. Let me give you a little background. In the beginning, when the Buddha was still alive, he traveled around India preaching the Dharma. The Buddha visited Sravasti, where Anathapindika did not often get to see the Buddha, whom he greatly admired. Anathapindika asked the Buddha to give him something by which to remember him. The Buddha gave him some of his fingernails and hair. Anathapindika then built a pagoda in which to commemorate these items and to make offerings to them. When the Buddha entered *parinirvana*, the eight kingdoms of India fought over his relics. Each kingdom built a pagoda, and these pagodas became known as the "eight great pagodas of India." This is how and when my career got off the ground.

Later, during the reign of King Asoka, who was the ruler of 84,000 kingdoms, the relics of the Buddha were collected and 84,000 pagodas were built. Since that time, building pagodas has been very popular. In China, there stands a pagoda in Yin County that many people believe was built by King Asoka. This is a huge mistake! Although King Asoka ruled 84,000 kingdoms, he never ruled China! How could he possibly have built the pagoda in Yin County? This mistake started with Qianchu, the King of Wuyueh, who greatly admired the 84,000 pagodas built by King Asoka. Those pagodas were made of silver, gold, and other metals, and each one contained a sutra. The misunderstanding probably started from here. Since this story relates to my country, let me explain in more detail.

Pagodas were first built in China when Sun Quan was the Emperor of the Eastern Wu kingdom during the Three Kingdoms Period. At that time, Emperor Sun Quan asked Master Kang Senghui the following question: "What teaching methods do you use?"

Master Kang Senghui replied, "I use Sakyamuni's teachings."

"Have the Tathagata's teachings come true?" asked the Emperor.

"The Buddha died more than a thousand years ago. His relics are found in many places. King Asoka built 84,000 pagodas in

which to house and venerate the relics of Buddha. This indicates that pagodas are built to honor the Tathagata's teachings," answered Master Kang Senghui.

Emperor Sun Quan then ordered Master Kang Senghui to look for relics and start building pagodas. This was why the first pagodas were built in China. Today, people are still building pagodas, but are they really doing so to honor the teachings of the Tathagata?

In fact, according to the Buddhist canon, only those edifices containing relics should be called pagodas. The others that do not contain relics should be called "columbaria." Out of respect for my noble status, I hope people will stop using the word "pagoda" as a general term for all towers. The true meaning will be lost if the wrong name is used.

Today, there are countless pagodas with different names, both in China and in Western countries. Some of their names are Three-Treasures Pagoda, Relic Pagoda, Patriarch Pagoda, Ordinary Pagoda, Robe and Alms-Bowl Pagoda, and Multi-Treasures Pagoda, to name just a few. Wherever I am built, that is where the Dharma is preached.

We pagodas are China's architectural treasures, standing alongside the great stone-carved statues of the Buddhas. Some of us pagodas are dozens of feet tall and rise so high that we reach right up into the clouds. Thousands of stone-carved Buddhas are found at the great ancient sites of Dunhuang, Yungang, and Longmen. The foreign visitors who come to see us at these sights lavishly praise the many contributions of Buddhism to Chinese culture!

Some poets have written verses regarding me, and the most popular one is the famous poem entitled "Pagoda." It is very simple and consists of only three lines.

> Here is the exquisite Linglong Pagoda.
> Linglong Pagoda is so exquisite.
> Thirteen stories has this exquisite pagoda.

I take these words as a big compliment, but some people running funeral services started using this poem. They would sing it in different tones to lament for the dead. Later on they even added more lines. Now the poem goes like this:

> Here is the exquisite Linglong Pagoda.
> Linglong Pagoda is so exquisite.
> Thirteen stories has the exquisite pagoda;
> Brass bells hang at every corner, tier upon tier.
> Hear the ding dong when the east breeze comes;
> The west wind changes the chime.

These changes not only make the poem sound vulgar and ordinary, but they also make a solemn Buddhist ritual sound like a folk song!

The person I dislike the most is a layperson from the Song dynasty who went by the name of Su Dongpo. He wrote about me in the following poem:

> The Yangtze River is a stick of ink.
> I hold Jiao Mountain in my hand to grind the
>   ink,
> The pagoda a big calligraphy brush.
> The sky is only wide enough to write eight lines.

From these verses, although I can tell that he has an exceptional mind and speech, he only sees me as a big calligraphy brush. I don't think this literary luminary truly knew the real me.

I have much more to talk to you about, but I don't want to keep you. I do want to remind all of you readers one last time that there are already plenty of renowned Buddhist pagodas around. We really shouldn't be worrying about building any new ones. Don't forget the saying that "saving just one human life is more beneficial than building a seven-story pagoda." In order for Buddhism to flourish, people need to give their support to educational, cultural, and charitable endeavors that benefit human beings directly. Doing this is worth more than building a thousand-storied pagoda. Building compassion in the hearts of people is the work of Buddhism, and it is also what is needed for these times.

Pagoda at Famen Temple, Shaanxi Province, China,
photograph courtesy of Fo Guang Shan Monastery

End Notes

1. Four imperial persecutions of Buddhism undertaken by emperors Taiwu of the Northern Wei dynasty (r. 423-452), Wu of the Northern Zhou dynasty (r. 560-578), Wuzong of Tang dynasty (r. 840-846), and Shizong of the Zhou dynasty (r. 954-959).

2. A military conflict between China and Japan on July 7, 1937, which lead to the second Sino-Japanese War.

3. Translated into English as "taking refuge in Amitabha Buddha," a common devotional chant used by Buddhists.

4. Sanskrit mantra associated with Avalokitesvara, the bodhisattva of compassion.

5. 1236-1283. One of the great national heroes of the Song dynasty who opposed the Mongol invaders.

6. 602-664. One of the most celebrated translators and scholars in the history of Chinese Buddhism, Xuanzang traveled to India to recover previously untranslated Buddhist texts. He recorded his journey in his *Record of Travels to the Western Regions*, which was later fictionalized in the classic Chinese novel *Journey to the West*.

7. r. 943–961

8. Annual Chinese holiday celebrated on the fifteenth day of the eighth lunar month. One main component of the celebration is the exchange of moon cakes.

9. Chinese strategy board game where players alternate placing black or white stones on a grid to capture and control territory. Also known by the Japanese name *go*.

10. Popular Chinese Buddhist ritual in which blessings are granted to living beings and the deceased by offering consecrated food.

11. One of the central protagonists of the classic Chinese novel *Journey to the West*.

12. r. 502-549. Known as a great patron of Buddhism, and creator of the Emperor Liang Repentance Service, a Buddhist repentance ceremony practiced to this day.

13. Similar to Chinese monastic robes, but made of thicker material. Arhat clothes include a medium-length robe that extends below the knee, but above the ankles.

14. 1890-1947. Chinese Buddhist reformer and forerunner of Humanistic Buddhism.

15. r. 1643-1661.

16. r. 690-705.

17. Robe worn by lay Buddhists for ceremonial purposes, such as during worship or repentence services.

18. r. 1661-1722.

19. A monastic appointed by the emperor to be the teacher of the imperial court and the nation.

20. In Chinese folklore, a red thread is said to connect two people who are destined to be lovers.

21. 638-713. Incredibly influential Chinese Chan Patriarch of which all extant Chan lineages derive. His teachings are preserved in the *Platform Sutra*.

22. Reference to an episode described in the *Suramgama Sutra* in which the Venerable Ananda is nearly seduced by a woman named Matangi due to an enchantment by her mother.

23. The predominant form of Buddhism practiced in Sri Lanka, Burma, Thailand, Laos, and parts of Vietnam. Monastics in these countries still gather alms daily.

24. Published in the early twentieth century and edited by Takakusu Junjiro, the *Taisho Tripitaka* is the edition of the Chinese Buddhist sutras and commentaries most frequently used and cited by modern scholars.

25. Wang Xiaoxu (1875-1948) and You Zhibiao (b.1901) were two prominent Chinese scientists who wrote Buddhist apologetics reconciling Buddhism and Science.

About the Author

Venerable Master Hsing Yun is a Chinese Buddhist monk, author, philanthropist, and founder of the Fo Guang Shan monastic order, which has branches throughout Asia, Europe, Africa, Australia, and the Americas. Ordained at the age of twelve in Jiangsu Province, China, Hsing Yun has spent over seventy years as a Buddhist monk promoting what he calls "Humanistic Buddhism"—Buddhism that meets the needs of people and is integrated into all aspects of daily life.

In 1949, Hsing Yun went to Taiwan and began to nurture the burgeoning Buddhist culture on the island. Early on in his monastic career, he was involved in promoting Buddhism through the written word. He has served as an editor and contributor for many Buddhist magazines and periodicals, authoring the daily columns "Between Ignorance and Enlightenment," "Dharma Words," and "Hsing Yun's Chan Talk." In 1957, he started his own Buddhist magazine, *Awakening the World*, and in 2000, the first daily Buddhist newspaper, the *Merit Times*.

Hsing Yun has authored more than one hundred books on how to bring happiness, peace, compassion and wisdom into daily life. These works include *Being Good*, *For All Living Beings*, and the *Rabbit's Horn*. He also edited and published the *Fo Guang Encyclopedia*, the most authoritative Buddhist reference work in the Chinese language. His contributions have reached as far as sponsoring Buddhist music and art to creating Buddhist programming for television, radio, and the stage.

Today Master Hsing Yun continues to travel around the world teaching the Dharma. In 2010 he delivered approximately 120 lectures and gave about 30 interviews for television and radio. He continues to write a daily column for the *Merit Times*, as well as to produce one-stroke calligraphy paintings. He is also the acting president of Buddha's Light International Association (BLIA), the worldwide lay Buddhist service organization.

About Buddha's Light Publishing

Buddha's Light Publishing offers quality translations of classical Buddhist texts as well as works by contemporary Buddhist teachers and scholars. We embrace Humanistic Buddhism, and promote Buddhist writing which is accessible, community-oriented, and relevant to daily life.

Founded in 1996 by Venerable Master Hsing Yun as the Fo Guang Shan International Translation Center, Buddha's Light Publishing seeks to continue Master Hsing Yun's goal of promoting the Buddha's teachings by fostering writing, art, and culture. Learn more by visiting www.blpusa.com.

Other Works by Venerable Master Hsing Yun:
After Many Autumns
Life
For All Living Beings
Being Good
Humanistic Buddhism: A Blueprint for Life
Chan Heart, Chan Art
Between Ignorance and Enlightenment Series

Sutra Commentaries:
Four Insights for Finding Fulfillment:
 A Practical Guide to the Buddha's Diamond Sutra
The Rabbit's Horn:
 A Commentary on the Platform Sutra
The Universal Gate:
 A Commentary on Avalokitesvara's Universal Gate Sutra
The Great Realizations:
 A Commentary on the Eight Realizations
 of a Bodhisattva Sutra
Sutra of the Medicine Buddha